Schummel

Zettel

ENGLISCH

Aufbau-wortschatz

Autumn Pierce

Sonderausgabe

Gestaltung: Carsten Abelbeck
Umschlaggestaltung: Inga Koch

ISBN 3-8174-5716-2
5157162

Vorwort

Das aktuelle und praktische Nachschlagewerk konzentriert sich auf das Wesentliche und behandelt die Bereiche, die erfahrungsgemäß wichtig sind und dem Lernenden häufig Probleme bereiten.

Der Aufbauwortschatz der englischen Sprache wird übersichtlich und systematisch dargestellt. Lautschriftangaben helfen dem Lernenden zur korrekten Aussprache der Wörter. Wichtige Tipps, Sonderfälle und Hinweise sind zum leichteren Auffinden durch Symbole und Hervorhebungen gekennzeichnet. Zahlreiche Beispielsätze verdeutlichen die Verwendungsmöglichkeiten und grammatischen Besonderheiten.

Erklärungen der Symbole:

 Falsche Freunde

 typische Fehlerquellen und nützliche Informationen zu Grammatik und Landeskunde

Alltagsleben (Hausrat, Kleidung)

1. Wohnen allgemein

air conditioning ['ɛəkəndɪʃənɪŋ]	Klimaanlage
Does the car come with air conditioning?	Hat das Auto eine Klimaanlage?
attic ['ætɪk]	Dachgeschoss
We store all our old things in the attic.	Wir lagern unsere alten Sachen im Dachgeschoss.
to budget ['bʌdʒɪt]	haushalten
You need to budget an extra 50 dollars a month for your English lessons.	Du musst jeden Monat 50 Dollar extra für deinen Englischunterricht einplanen.
caretaker ['kɛəteɪkə]	Hausmeister(in)
cellar ['selə]	Keller
Her parents have a large wine cellar.	Ihre Eltern haben einen großen Weinkeller.
chimney ['tʃɪmnɪ]	Schornstein
cleaner ['kliːnə]	Raumpfleger(in)
dining room ['daɪnɪŋ ruːm]	Esszimmer
We only eat in the dining room when we have guests.	Wir essen nur im Esszimmer, wenn wir Gäste haben.
double glazing ['dʌbl 'gleɪzɪŋ]	Doppelfenster

fence [fens] — Zaun

The verb *to fence* refers to the traditional sport with swords (German: *fechten*).

heater ['hiːtə] — Heizkörper
Please, don't put any fabrics near the heater! — Leg bitte keine Stoffe in die Nähe des Heizkörpers!

heating ['hiːtɪŋ] — Heizung
Who turned the heating down? — Wer hat die Heizung heruntergedreht?

hedge [hedʒ] — Hecke
We need to trim the hedge. — Wir müssen die Hecke schneiden.

litter ['lɪtə] — Abfall
That used to be a lovely park, but now it is full of litter. — Dies war einst ein schöner Park, aber jetzt ist er voll mit Abfall.

living room ['lɪvɪŋ ruːm] — Wohnzimmer
They are watching TV in the living room. — Sie schauen im Wohnzimmer fern.

radiator ['reɪdɪeɪtə] — Heizkörper

rent [rent] — Miete
She was evicted from the apartment for not paying her monthly rent. — Sie ist aus der Wohnung geflogen, weil sie ihre Monatsmiete nicht gezahlt hat.

While in Germany, there is a difference between *Kalt-* and *Warmmiete*, in the US and England rent usually does not include heating, electricity etc. These services are known as *utilities* and are always paid separately to the different providers.

rubbish ['rʌbɪʃ] — Abfall

The word *rubbish* can be used when you want to describe something negatively.
Ex: That movie was rubbish.
Der Film war schlecht.
He told me a load of rubbish.
Er hat mir eine Menge Quatsch erzählt.

suburb ['sʌbɜːb] — Vorort

Household verbs and expressions
to take out the rubbish: den Müll wegbringen
to do the dishes: den Abwasch machen
to vacuum: staubsaugen
to move in: einziehen
to move out: ausziehen
to pay the rent: die Miete zahlen
to tidy one's room: das Zimmer aufräumen
to sweep the floor: den Boden fegen
to do the spring cleaning: den Frühlingsputz machen

2. Einrichtungsgegenstände

ashtray ['æʃtreɪ]	Aschenbecher
bedclothes ['bedkləʊðz]	Bettwäsche
The beds upstairs need fresh bedclothes.	Die Betten oben brauchen frische Bettwäsche.

Types of bedclothes
pillow: Kopfkissen
pillow case: Kopfkissenhülle
sheet: Betttuch
cover: Decke

bookcase ['bʊkkeɪs]	Bücherregal
We moved the bookcase into the study.	Wir haben das Bücherregal ins Arbeitszimmer gestellt.
candle ['kændl]	Kerze

Idioms with candle
burn the candle at both ends: sehr hart arbeiten
to hold a candle to: vergleichbar sein mit
Ex: Her cake cannot hold a candle to mine.
Ihr Kuchen ist nicht so gut wie meiner.

candle stick ['kændl 'stɪk]	Kerzenständer
She hurt him with the candle stick.	Sie verletzte ihn mit dem Kerzenständer.

carpet ['kɑːpət]	Teppich
The carpet seems to be mouldy.	Der Teppich scheint schimmelig zu sein.
coat hanger [kəʊt 'hæŋgə]	Kleiderbügel
The coat hangers are in the hall closet.	Die Kleiderbügel befinden sich in dem Wandschrank im Gang.
cupboard ['kʌbəd]	Schrank
Put the dishes into the cupboard.	Räum das Geschirr in den Schrank.

Closet and cupboard

In German, the word *Schrank* is the translation for both *closet* and *cupboard*. There is a difference in English. A *closet* refers to an actual space built into a wall. *Closets* are usually used for storing clothing and shoes. *Cupboards*, on the other hand, are movable pieces of furniture with shelves and doors. Usually, dishes and food are stored in *cupboards*.

flower pot ['flaʊə pɔt]	Blumentopf
Three of our flower pots are broken.	Drei unserer Blumentöpfe sind zerbrochen.
house plant [haʊs plɑːnt]	Zimmerpflanze

Other uses of plant

to plant a tree: einen Baum pflanzen
power plant: Kraftwerk

iron ['aɪən]	Bügeleisen
Whose turn is it to do the ironing?	Wer ist mit dem Bügeln dran?
He even irons his jeans!	Er bügelt sogar seine Jeans!
ironing board ['aɪənɪŋ bɔːd]	Bügelbrett
jug [dʒʌg]	Krug
The jugs were full of water.	Die Krüge waren voll Wasser.
lamp-shade [læmp ʃeɪd]	Lampenschirm
The lamp-shade is dusty.	Der Lampenschirm ist staubig.
picture frame ['pɪktʃə freɪm]	Bilderrahmen
The picture frame is an antique.	Der Bilderrahmen ist eine Antiquität.
potted plant [pɔtɪd plɑːnt]	Topfpflanze
pram [præm]	Kinderwagen

In American English, *a pram* is called *a stroller*, *a buggy* or *a baby carriage*.

quilt [kwɪlt]	Federbett; Decke
My grandmother made that quilt.	Meine Oma hat diese Flickendecke gemacht.
rug [rʌg]	Läufer
tablecloth ['teɪblkɔθ]	Tischdecke
The tablecloth is made of linen.	Die Tischdecke ist aus Leinen.

vacuum cleaner ['vækjʊəm 'kliːnə]	Staubsauger
The vacuum cleaner is so loud I can't think any more.	Der Staubsauger ist so laut, dass ich nicht mehr denken kann.

Idioms with household items

to iron things out: Probleme klären
Ex: The couple managed to iron things out and are happier than ever.
to cut a rug: eifrig tanzen
Ex: Sarah's grandparents really cut a rug at her party.
to frame someone: jemanden hereinlegen.
Ex: He was framed for murder.

vase [vɑːz]	Blumenvase
The cat knocked over the vase.	Die Katze schmiss die Vase um.
watering can ['wɔːtərɪŋ kæn]	Gießkanne

Verbs for household items

to turn on the light: das Licht anmachen
to pot: eintopfen
to push a pram: einen Kinderwagen schieben
to water the flowers: die Blumen gießen
to make the bed: das Bett machen
to dust: Staub wischen
to set the table: den Tisch decken

3. Küche und Essen

coaster ['kaʊstə] — Untersetzer
Please put a coaster under your glass, or the table will be ruined. — Bitte nimm einen Untersetzer unter dein Glas, sonst wird der Tisch beschädigt.

crockery ['krɔkərɪ] — Geschirr
cutlery ['kʌtlərɪ] — Besteck
cutlet ['kʌtlɪt] — Schnitzel
cut loaf ['kʌt'ləʊf] — aufgeschnittenes Brot
cuttlefish ['kʌtlfɪʃ] — Tintenfisch
diet ['daɪət] — Diät
My mother is always on a diet. — Meine Mutter macht ständig Diät.

Diet words
calorie: Kalorie
fat: Fett
scales: Waage
to lose weight: abnehmen
to gain weight: zunehmen

egg cup [eg kʌp] — Eierbecher
freezer ['fri:zə] — Gefriertruhe
We have plenty of ice-cream in the freezer. — Wir haben viel Eiskrem in der Gefriertruhe.
fridge [frɪdʒ] — Kühlschrank

Unfortunately I have no food in my fridge (refridgerator).
Ich habe leider nichts zu essen in meinem Kühlschrank.

frying pan ['fraɪɪŋ pæn]
Pfanne

Idiom
out of the frying pan into the fire
vom Regen in die Traufe kommen

kettle ['ketl]
Wasserkessel

If you want tea, the kettle is already boiling.
Das Wasser kocht schon, falls du jetzt Tee möchtest.

saucepan ['sɔːspən]
Kochtopf

There is still some soup in the saucepan.
Es ist noch Suppe im Kochtopf.

serviette [sɜːvɪ'et]
Serviette

sink [sɪnk]
Spüle

Put the dishes in the sink!
Räum das Geschirr in die Spüle!

tea pot [tiː pɔt]
Teekanne

Use the porcelain tea pot!
Nimm die Teekanne aus Porzellan!

tea towel [tiː taʊl]
Geschirrtuch

Where have all our tea towels gone?
Wo sind all unsere Geschirrtücher geblieben?

thermos flask ['θɜːməs flɑːsk]
Thermosflasche

He always takes a thermos flask of coffee to work. — Er nimmt immer eine Thermosflasche Kaffee mit in die Arbeit.

tin opener [tɪn 'əʊpenə] — Dosenöffner

tissues ['tɪʃuːz] — Papiertücher

I used up so many tissues when I had a cold. — Als ich erkältet war, habe ich sehr viele Papiertücher aufgebraucht.

washing-up liquid ['wɔʃɪŋ ʌp 'lɪkwɪd] — Spülmittel

Kitchen and eating

British	*American*
crockery	dishes
cutlery	silverware
serviette	napkin
tea towel	dish towel
washing up liquid	diswashing liquid/soap

4. Bad und Reinigen

after-shave ['ɑːftə ʃeɪv] — Rasierwasser

Have you been using a new after-shave? — Benutzt du ein neues Rasierwasser?

cloth [klɔθ] — Wischlappen

I need a cloth to wipe up the milk. — Ich brauche einen Lappen, um die Milch wegzuwischen.

clothes line [kləʊðz laɪn]	Wäscheleine
clothes peg [kləʊðz peg]	Wäscheklammer
I am out of clothes pegs.	Mir sind die Wäscheklammern ausgegangen.
comb [kəʊm]	Kamm

Other words with the silent b

thumb: Daumen
numb: betäubt
door jamb: Türrahmen

deodorant [dɪ'əʊdərənt]	Deo
disinfectant [dɪsən'fektənt]	Desinfektionsmittel
The hospital smells of disinfectant.	Das Krankenhaus riecht nach Desinfektionsmittel.
floor polish [flɔː 'pɔlɪʃ]	Bohnerwachs
flannel ['flænl]	Waschlappen
hairbrush ['hɛə brʌʃ]	Haarbürste
Your hairbrush is in your handbag.	Deine Haarbürste ist in deiner Handtasche.
hair conditioner [hɛə kən'dɪʃənə]	Haarkur; Pflegespülung
I use conditioner every other day.	Ich benutze jeden zweiten Tag eine Pflegespülung.
hair-dryer ['hɛə 'draɪə]	Föhn
Stay away from the bath with the hair-dryer!	Bleib mit dem Föhn von der Badewanne weg!
nail file [neɪlfaɪl]	Nagelfeile

I've broken a nail. Do you have a nail file?	Ich habe einen Nagel gebrochen. Hast du eine Nagelfeile?
to polish ['pɔlɪʃ]	bohnern; polieren
We polish the silver every week.	Wir polieren das Silber jede Woche.
razor ['reɪzə]	Rasierapparat; Rasiermesser
electric razor	Elektrorasierer
razor blade ['reɪzə bleɪd]	Rasierklinge
The razor blade is blunt.	Die Rasierklinge ist stumpf.
scissors ['sɪzəz]	Schere
a pair of scissors	eine Schere
shampoo [ʃæm'puː]	Shampoo
I don't like the smell of men's shampoo.	Ich mag den Geruch von Männershampoo nicht.
shaving cream ['ʃeɪvɪŋ kriːm]	Rasierschaum
You have shaving cream on your cheek.	Du hast Rasierschaum auf der Wange.
shoe polish [ʃuː 'pɔlɪʃ]	Schuhkrem
I need black shoe polish for my shoes.	Ich brauche schwarze Schuhkrem für meine Schuhe.
sponge [spʌndʒ]	Schwamm
toilet paper ['tɔɪlət 'peɪpə]	Toilettenpapier
Could you get a new roll of toilet paper?	Könntest du eine neue Rolle Toilettenpapier holen?

towel [taʊl]	Handtuch
Where are the guest towels?	Wo sind die Gästehandtücher?
towel rail	Handtuchhalter
washbasin ['wɔʃbeɪsən]	Waschbecken
He always leaves toothpaste in the washbasin.	Er hinterlässt immer Zahnpasta im Waschbecken.
washing machine ['wɔʃɪŋ mə'ʃiːn]	Waschmaschine
The washing machine is not pumping the water.	Die Waschmaschine pumpt das Wasser nicht ab.
washing powder ['wɔʃɪŋ 'paʊdə]	Waschpulver

Useful verbs

to brush one's hair: sich die Haare bürsten
to wash one's hair: sich die Haare waschen
to shave: sich rasieren
to take a shower: sich duschen
to dry oneself: sich abtrocknen
to brush one's teeth: sich die Zähne putzen
to dry one's hair: sich die Haare föhnen
to put on make-up: sich schminken
to wash one's hands: sich die Hände waschen
to take off one's make-up: sich abschminken
to powder: pudern

5. Kleidung, Accessoires und Kosmetik

accessories [ək'sesərɪz]
Zubehör; Accessoires

The hair-dryer comes with several accessories.
Der Föhn kommt mit verschiedenem Zubehör.

What accessories are you going to wear with that dress?
Welche Accessoires wirst du zu diesem Kleid tragen?

apron ['eɪprən]
Schürze

He looks funny when he wears his checked apron.
Er sieht lustig aus, wenn er seine karierte Schürze trägt.

In English a *Schürzenjäger* is not translated into an apron hunter. You can call a man who chases the ladies a *womanizer* or a *ladykiller*.

body ['bɔdɪ]
Body

I often wear a body in the winter to keep warm.
Ich trage im Winter oft einen Body, um mich warm zu halten.

bow tie [bəʊ taɪ]
Fliege

A bow tie is an alternative to a tie.
Eine Fliege ist eine Alternative zur Krawatte.

bra [brɑː]
BH

brooch [brəʊtʃ]
Brosche

That brooch belonged to my grandmother.
Diese Brosche gehörte meiner Großmutter.

buckle ['bʌkl]	Schnalle
The buckle is broken.	Die Schnalle ist kaputt.
button ['bʌtən]	Knopf
The child's coat is missing two buttons.	An der Jacke des Kindes fehlen zwei Knöpfe.
cardigan ['kɑːdɪgən]	Strickjacke
Old men often wear cardigans.	Alte Männer tragen öfters Strickjacken.
chain [tʃeɪn]	Kette
Her chain is made of silver.	Ihre Kette ist aus Silber.
cosmetics [kɔz'metɪks]	Kosmetika
She doesn't use as many cosmetics as before.	Sie benutzt weniger Kosmetika als früher.
cuff-links [kʌf lɪŋks]	Manschetten
He has cuff-links with his family crest.	Er hat Manschetten mit seinem Familienwappen.
dressing gown ['dresɪŋ gaʊn]	Bademantel
She answered the door in her dressing gown.	Sie ist, nur mit einem Bademantel bekleidet, an die Tür gegangen.
earrings ['ɪərɪŋz]	Ohrringe
eye shadow [aɪ 'ʃædəʊ]	Lidschatten
Green eye shadow looks terrible on her.	Grüner Lidschatten steht ihr überhaupt nicht.
foundation [faʊn'deɪʃən]	Grundierungskrem
I only use foundation when I have spots.	Ich benutze Tönungskrem nur, wenn ich Pickel habe.

glove [glʌv]	Handschuh

Idioms with glove

to be hand in glove with someone: mit jemandem sehr eng befreundet sein

Ex: She is hand in glove with the chairman of the board.

to fit like a glove: ganz genau passen

Ex: My new coat fits me like a glove.

handbag ['hændbæg]	Handtasche
Her new handbag is by Prenda.	Ihre neue Handtasche ist von Prenda.
heels [hiːlz]	Absätze
She thinks high heels are uncomfortable.	Sie findet hohe Absätze unbequem.
jewellery ['dʒuːlrɪ]	Schmuck
The family has a fine collection of antique jewellery.	Die Familie ist im Besitz einer schönen Sammlung antiken Schmucks.
knee-highs [niː haɪz]	Kniestrümpfe
mascara [mə'skɑːra]	Wimperntusche
She only uses water-proof mascara.	Sie benutzt nur wasserfeste Wimperntusche.
moisturizer ['mɔɪstʃəraɪzə]	Feuchtigkeitskrem
It is important to use moisturizer if you don't want wrinkles.	Es ist wichtig, eine Feuchtigkeitskrem zu verwenden, wenn du Falten vermeiden willst.

nappy ['næpɪ]	Windel
The American word for nappy is diaper.	Das amerikanische Wort für Windel heißt „diaper".
panties ['pæntiːz]	Höschen
perfume ['pɜːfjuːm]	Parfüm
perm [pɜːm]	Dauerwelle
She must have got a perm. Her hair used to be straight.	Sie muss sich eine Dauerwelle gemacht haben lassen. Ihre Haare waren glatt.
raincoat ['reɪnkəʊt]	Regenmantel
Take your raincoat if you go to London!	Nimm deinen Regenmantel mit, falls du nach London fährst!
safety pin ['seɪftɪ pɪn]	Sicherheitsnadel
The safety pin pricked his skin.	Die Sicherheitsnadel pikste in seine Haut.
sandals ['sændəlz]	Sandalen

Clothing, accessories and cosmetics synonyms

body: bodysuit
brooch: pin
cosmetics: make-up
stockings: nylons
suspenders (Strapse): garters
waistcoat: vest
wallet: billfold
handbag: purse
washing: laundry

scarf [skɑːf]	Halstuch; Schal
She always has beautiful silk scarves.	Sie hat immer schöne Seidenhalstücher.
shawl [ʃɔːl]	Schal; Umschlagtuch
shoe lace [ʃuː leɪs]	Schnürsenkel
slippers ['slɪpəz]	Pantoffeln
I love fluffy slippers.	Ich liebe flauschige Pantoffeln.
stockings ['stɔkɪŋz]	Strümpfe
She only wears black stockings.	Sie trägt nur schwarze Strümpfe.
sunblock ['sʌnblɔk]	Sonnenschutzkrem
You should always use sunblock, even on cloudy days.	Du solltest immer Sonnenschutzkrem benutzen, auch an bedeckten Tagen.
sunglasses ['sʌnglɑːsɪz]	Sonnenbrille
suspenders [sə'spendəz]	Hosenträger; Strapse
Clowns often wear baggy pants with suspenders.	Clowns tragen oft weite Hosen mit Hosenträgern.
Her dress was so short that you could see her suspenders.	Ihr Kleid war so kurz, dass man ihre Strapse sehen konnte.
sweater ['swetə]	Pullover

sweater vs. jumper

In American English, a *Pullover* is called a *sweater*. In British English, a pullover is called *a jumper*. But in American English, a jumper is the German equivalent of a *Latzhose*!

tie pin [taɪ pɪn]	Krawattennadel
toner ['təʊnə]	Gesichtswasser
Every night I use soap followed by a toner.	Jeden Abend benutze ich Seife und Gesichtswasser.
umbrella [ʌm'brelə]	Regenschirm
I left my umbrella on the tube.	Ich habe meinen Regenschirm in der U-Bahn vergessen.
underwear ['ʌndəwɛə]	Unterwäsche
She was embarrassed about being caught in her underwear.	Es war ihr peinlich, in Unterwäsche erwischt zu werden.
waistcoat ['weɪstkəʊt]	Weste
wallet ['wɔlət]	Brieftasche
His wallet was stolen in Madrid.	In Madrid wurde ihm die Brieftasche geklaut.
washing ['wɔʃɪŋ]	Wäsche
John does the washing every weekend.	John macht die Wäsche jedes Wochenende.
wellingtons ['welɪŋtənz]	Gummistiefel
Take your wellingtons when you go for a walk on the field!	Nimm deine Gummistiefel mit, wenn du auf der Wiese spazieren gehst!
winter boots ['wɪntə buːts]	Winterstiefel
Her winter boots are lined with fur.	Ihre Winterstiefel sind mit Pelz gefüttert.
winter coat ['wɪntə kəʊt]	Wintermantel
zip [zɪp]	Reißverschluss

The zip on her jeans is open. — Der Reißverschluss ihrer Jeans ist offen.

6. Heimwerken

to drill [drɪl] — bohren
He drilled holes for the new shelves. — Er bohrte Löcher für die neuen Regale.
to drill down — in die Tiefe bohren
They drilled down 600 feet. — Sie bohrten in eine Tiefe von 600 Fuß.

drill [drɪl] — Bohrer; Bohrmaschine

False Friends
To bore in English means *jemanden langweilen*! Ex:
His story bored me to death.
Seine Geschichte hat mich zu Tode gelangweilt.

file [faɪl] — Feile; *v* feilen
to file away — abfeilen
to file down — abfeilen
glue [gluː] — Klebstoff; kleben
I need some glue to repair the vase. — Ich brauche etwas Klebstoff, um die Vase zu reparieren.

He glued the pieces of the vase together. — Er klebte die Bruchstücke der Vase zusammen.
light bulb [laɪt bʌlb] — Glühbirne

The light bulb in the bathroom has gone. — Die Glühbirne im Badezimmer ist durchgebrannt.

monkey wrench ['mʌnkɪ rentʃ] — Engländer; Universalschlüssel; Schraubenschlüssel

nail [neɪl] — Nagel

Chris missed the nail and hit his finger instead. — Chris verfehlte den Nagel und erwischte stattdessen seinen Finger.

to plane [pleɪn] — hobeln

plane [pleɪn] — Hobel

plug [plʌg] — Dübel

to saw [sɔː] — sägen

He sawed the boards. — Er sägte die Bretter.

Tool idioms

to drill someone: jemanden ausfragen
Ex: She drilled her son in French.
Sie fragte ihren Sohn in Französisch aus.
to have a screw loose:
eine Schraube locker haben
Ex: Ever since the accident, she has had a screw loose.
Seit dem Unfall hat sie eine Schraube locker.
to hit the nail on the head: ein Volltreffer landen
to nail someone: jemanden erwischen; verhaften
Ex: She nailed him as he was leaving with the car.
Sie hat ihn erwischt, als er mit dem Auto wegfahren wollte.

saw [sɔː] — Säge

screw [skruː]	Schraube; schrauben
We need one more screw for the shelf.	Wir brauchen noch eine Schraube für das Regal.
Can you screw in the light bulb?	Kannst du die Glühbirne hineinschrauben?
screw-driver [skruː 'draɪvə]	Schraubenzieher
sellotape ['selәteɪp]	Tesafilm
Sellotape is not strong enough.	Tesafilm ist nicht stark genug.
tape measure [teɪp 'meʒə]	Maßband
We need a tape measure to see exactly how wide it is.	Wir brauchen ein Maßband, um die genaue Breite festzustellen.
tool kit [tuːl kɪt]	Werkzeugkasten
tools [tuːlz]	Werkzeug
vice [vaɪs]	Schraubstock

False Friends

In English, *a vice* has the same meaning as *Laster* (im Sinne von Sucht; Sünde) in German.

white wash [waɪt wɔʃ]	Tünche

Irregular past tense

to take out the rubbish: He took out the rubbish.
to get dressed: She got up and got dressed.
to run the dishwasher: The children ran the dishwasher.
to eat breakfast: My mother ate breakfast.

to sit at the table: They sat at the table.
to go to sleep: He went to sleep early.
to sleep late: Mike slept late.
to fall down the stairs: He fell down the stairs.

Informatik

access ['ækses]	Zugriff
You do not have access to that file.	Du hast keinen Zugriff auf diese Datei.
I tried to access that file.	Ich habe versucht, auf jene Datei zuzugreifen.
application [æplɪ'keɪʃən]	Anwendung
It includes all standard applications.	Alle Standardanwendungen sind enthalten.
backup ['bækʌp]	Back-up; Reserve; Sicherheitssystem
He forgot to make a backup of the database.	Er vergaß, eine Sicherheitskopie der Datenbank zu machen.
bar code [bɑː kəʊd]	Strichcode
basic mode ['beɪsɪk məʊd]	Basismodus
binary ['baɪnərɪ]	binär
A binary system is based on the numbers 1 and 0.	Ein Binärsystem basiert auf den Zahlen 1 und 0.
binary number ['baɪnərɪ 'nʌmbə]	Binärzahl

bit [bɪt]	Bit
to boot [buːt]	laden
Try to boot the program again!	Versuche, das Programm noch einmal zu laden!
browser ['braʊsə]	Browser
Always close your browser after finishing internet banking.	Schließ immer den Browser, wenn du mit dem Onlinebanking fertig bist.
bug [bʌg]	Fehler
The system has a bug.	Das System hat einen Fehler.
byte [baɪt]	Byte
to cancel ['kænsəl]	löschen
CD-ROM [siːdiː'rɔm]	CD-ROM
character ['kærəktə]	Zeichen
You can enter up to 50 characters.	Du kannst bis zu 50 Zeichen eingeben.
chat [tʃæt]	Chat (Konversation via Computer)

Different keyboards

If you are using an English keyboard, you may be in for a few surprises. First, the positions of the Z and the Y keys are reversed, since Y is used more often in the English language than Z. Also, there are no separate keys for *Umlaute*. Instead, they are located under the Symbols *(Sonderzeichen)* and must be selected and inserted.

chip [tʃɪp]	Chip
to click [klɪk]	klicken
He clicked on the link, but nothing happened.	Er klickte auf den Link, aber nichts passierte.
code [kəʊd]	Code
to code [kəʊd]	kodieren
command [kə'maːnd]	Befehl
He entered the command to reboot.	Er gab den Befehl zum Neustart ein.
compatible [kəm'pætɪbl]	kompatibel; vereinbar
Those two systems are not compatible.	Diese beiden Systeme sind nicht kompatibel.
computer [kəm'pjuːtə]	Computer; Rechner
computer equipment [kəm'pjuːtə ɪ'kwɪpmənt]	EDV-Anlage
configuration [kɔnfɪgə'reɪʃən]	Konfiguration
Check and see if the configuration is correct.	Überprüfen Sie, ob die Konfiguration stimmt.
console ['kɔnsəʊl]	Steuerpult
to control [kən'trəʊl]	steuern
You can control all the processes using this function.	Du kannst mit dieser Funktion alle Prozesse steuern.
control [kən'trɔʊl]	Steuerung
to convert [kən'vɜːt]	konvertieren
Can you convert the document to a plain text file?	Könnten Sie das Dokument in eine einfache Text-Datei konvertieren?

crash [kræʃ]	Absturz
My computer crashed twice yesterday.	Mein Computer stürzte gestern zweimal ab.
cursor ['kɜːsə]	Cursor; Mauszeiger
cyberspace ['saɪbəspeɪs]	Cyberspace
data ['deɪtə]	Daten
database ['deɪtəbeɪs]	Datenbank
The database contains all the information about our customers.	Die Datenbank enthält alle Informationen über unsere Kunden.
data entry ['deɪtə 'entrɪ]	Dateneingabe
data processing ['deɪtə 'prəʊsesɪŋ]	Datenverarbeitung
debugging [diː'bʌgɪŋ]	Fehlersuche und Fehlerbeseitigung
to delete [dɪ'liːt]	löschen
Please delete all the files you don't need any more.	Bitte löschen Sie alle Dateien, die Sie nicht mehr brauchen.
desktop publishing ['desktɔp 'pʌblɪʃɪŋ]	Desktop-Publishing
directory [dɪ'rektərɪ]	(Datei)Verzeichnis; Ordner
disk [dɪsk]	Platte; Diskette
The hard disk is damaged.	Die Festplatte ist geschädigt.
Can you lend me a disk?	Kannst du mir eine Diskette leihen?

disk drive ['dıskdraıv]	Laufwerk
diskette [dıs'ket]	Diskette
display unit [dıs'pleı 'juːnıt]	Bildschirm
The display unit is flickering.	Der Bildschirm flackert.
document ['dɔkjʊmənt]	Dokument
drive [draıv]	Laufwerk
My new computer has a DVD drive.	Mein neuer Computer hat ein DVD-Laufwerk.
electronic data processing (EDP) [ılək'trɔnık 'deıtə 'prəʊsesıŋ]	elektronische Datenverarbeitung (EDV)
e-mail ['iːmeıl]	E-Mail
I will send you the document via e-mail.	Ich werde dir das Dokument per E-Mail zukommen lassen.

E-mail words

attachment: Anhang
Cc (Copy): Kopie
Bcc (Blind Copy): blinde Kopie
signature: Unterschrift
subject: Betreffzeile
mailing list: Verteilerliste
body: Textfeld
settings: Einstellungen

to enter ['entə]	eingeben
Please enter your password!	Bitte geben Sie Ihr Passwort ein!
entry ['entrı]	Eingabe
The entry was incorrect.	Die Eingabe war falsch.

to erase [ɪ'reɪz]	löschen
The virus erased everything.	Der Virus löschte alles.
field [fiːld]	Feld
file [faɪl]	Datei
file name ['faɪl neɪm]	Dateiname
Two files shouldn't have the same file name.	Zwei Dateien sollten nicht denselben Dateinamen haben.
to format ['fɔːmæt]	formatieren
The disk has already been formatted.	Die Diskette wurde bereits formatiert.
format ['fɔːmæt]	Format
hacker ['hækə]	Hacker
hard copy [hɑːd 'kɔpɪ]	gedruckte Bildschirmseite; Ausdruck
Can you give her a hard copy of the presentation?	Kannst du ihr einen Ausdruck der Präsentation geben?
hard disk [hɑːd dɪsk]	Festplatte
hardware ['hɑːdwɛə]	Hardware
high-resolution [haɪ rezə'luːʃən]	(mit) hohe(r) Auflösung
hyperlink ['haɪpəliŋk]	Hyperlink
homepage [həumpeɪdʒ]	Homepage
His homepage is very creative.	Seine Homepage ist sehr kreativ.
information science [ɪnfə'meɪʃən 'saɪəns]	Informatik

Information science is also known as computer science.	Informatik ist auch unter Computerwissenschaft bekannt.
to initialize [ɪ'nɪʃəlaɪz]	initialisieren; formatieren
input ['ɪnpʊt]	Eingabe
to install [ɪn'stɔːl]	einbauen; installieren
I installed a new system yesterday.	Ich habe gestern ein neues System installiert.
interactive [ɪntə'æktɪv]	interaktiv
interface ['ɪntəfeɪs]	Schnittstelle
Internet ['ɪntənet]	Internet
He spends a lot of time surfing the Internet.	Er verbringt viel Zeit beim Surfen im Internet.
key [kiː]	Taste

Computer keys

delete: löschen
scroll: Bild
insert: einfügen
control: Steuerung
return: Eingabe

keyboard ['kiːbɔːd]	Tastatur
I spilled water on my keyboard, but it still worked. Thank God!	Ich habe Wasser auf meine Tastatur gekippt, aber sie hat Gott sei Dank noch funktioniert.
keyword ['kiːwɜːd]	Passwort; Kennwort
We change our keywords every month.	Wir ändern unsere Passwörter jeden Monat.

laptop ['læptɔp]	Laptop
laser printer ['leɪzə 'prɪntə]	Laserdrucker
The laser printer is out of toner.	Dem Laserdrucker ist der Toner ausgegangen.
linkage ['lɪŋkɪdʒ]	Verbindung
to load [ləʊd]	laden
Let's load some new games.	Lass uns ein paar neue Spiele laden.
to log in [lɔg ɪn]	einloggen
memory ['meməri]	Speicherkapazität
My computer has no memory left.	Mein Computer hat keine Speicherkapazität mehr.
menu ['menjuː]	Menü
microprocessor ['maɪkrəʊ'prəʊsesə]	Mikroprozessor
modem ['məʊdəm]	Modem
I have a modem for the Internet and for the fax machine.	Ich habe ein Modem für das Internet und für das Faxgerät.
monitor ['mɔnɪtə]	Monitor
mouse [maʊs]	Maus
Use the right mouse button!	Klick auf die rechte Maustaste!
network ['netwɜːk]	Netzwerk
offline ['ɔflaɪn]	offline
I am going to work offline today.	Ich werde heute offline arbeiten.
online ['ɔnlaɪn]	online

I was online for two hours last night.	Ich war gestern Nacht zwei Stunden lang online.
operating system ['ɔpəreɪtɪŋ 'sɪstəm]	Betriebssystem
Many experts recommend the Linux operating system.	Viele Experte empfehlen das Linux Betriebssystem.
password ['pɑːswɜːd]	Passwort; Kennwort
PC (personal computer) ['piːsiː]	PC (Personalcomputer)
printer ['prɪntə]	Drucker; Printer
The printer is out of paper.	Der Drucker hat kein Papier mehr.
to process ['prəʊses]	verarbeiten
The computer needs half an hour to process the data.	Der Rechner braucht eine halbe Stunde, um die Daten zu verarbeiten.
processing ['prəʊsesɪŋ]	Verarbeitung
The processing is slow.	Die Verarbeitung geht langsam.
processor ['prəʊsesə]	Prozessor
program ['prəʊgræm]	Programm
What can that program do?	Was kann dieses Programm?
programmer ['prəʊgræmə]	Programmierer(in)
He is working as a free-lance programmer.	Er arbeitet als selbstständiger Programmierer.
to retrieve [rɪ'triːv]	abrufen; aufrufen
to retrieve a file	eine Datei aufrufen

Can you retrieve the file?	Kannst du die Datei noch aufrufen?
to save [seɪv]	abspeichern
I save my document every ten minutes.	Ich speichere meine Datei alle zehn Minuten ab.
saving ['seɪvɪŋ]	Abspeicherung
scanner ['skænə]	Scanner
He used the scanner to put the pictures in a digital format.	Er benutzte den Scanner, um die Bilder in ein digitales Format zu bringen.
screen [skriːn]	Bildschirm
server ['sɜːvə]	Server
The server has been down for two days.	Der Server funktioniert seit zwei Tagen nicht mehr.
software ['sɔftwɛə]	Software
to sort [sɔːt]	sortieren
I need to sort the files.	Ich muss die Dateien sortieren.
special character ['speʃəl 'kærəktə]	Sonderzeichen
You can find it under special characters.	Du findest es unter Sonderzeichen.
storage ['stɔːrɪdʒ]	Speicher; Speicherplatz
The storage limit on my computer has been reached.	Das Speicherplatzlimit auf meinem Computer wurde erreicht.
storage capacity [stɔːrɪdʒ kə'pæsətɪ]	Speicherkapazität

to store [stɔː]	abspeichern
telecommuting ['telɪkəmjuːtɪŋ]	Telearbeit
Jolene has been telecommuting since she had the baby.	Seitdem Jolene das Baby hat, macht sie Telearbeit.
user ['juːzə]	Anwender(in)
Not every user has access to the private data.	Nicht jeder Benutzer hat Zugriff auf die privaten Daten.
user-friendly ['juːzə 'frendlɪ]	benutzerfreundlich
I found the old program more user-friendly.	Ich fand das alte Programm benutzerfreundlicher.
virus ['vaɪrəs]	Virus
Look out for viruses sent in e-mails.	Pass auf Viren auf, die über E-Mails verschickt werden.
web site [web saɪt]	Web-Site; Web-Seite
window ['wɪndəʊ]	Fenster
word processing [wɜːd 'prəʊsesɪŋ]	Textverarbeitung
We need a better word processing program.	Wir brauchen ein besseres Textverarbeitungsprogramm.
World Wide Web (WWW) [wɜːld waɪd web]	World Wide Web

Kunst

1. Kunst allgemein und Kunstgeschichte

abstract ['æbstrækt]	abstrakt
That picture is very abstract.	Das Gemälde ist sehr abstrakt.
art collection [ɑːt kə'lekʃən]	Kunstsammlung
The family's art collection is centuries old.	Die Kunstsammlung der Familie ist Jahrhunderte alt.

False Friends

Watch out!

Art and the German *Art* are not the same. *Art* in English means *Kunst* in German. *Die Art* translated into English would be *type* or *sort*.

Ex: Ich mag diese Art von Musik nicht.

I don't like this type of music.

art critic [ɑːt 'krɪtɪk]	Kunstkritiker
He studied art history and is now working as an art critic.	Er hat Kunstgeschichte studiert und arbeitet jetzt als Kunstkritiker.
artist [ɑːtɪst]	Künstler(in)
artistic [ɑːtɪstɪk]	künstlerisch; kunstverständig

She has an artistic nature.	Sie hat eine künstlerische Natur.
avant-garde [ævɔŋ'gɑːd]	Avantgarde
They were part of the avant-garde movement.	Sie waren Mitglieder der Avantgardebewegung.
Baroque [bə'rɔk]	Barock
Baroque architecture is very ornate.	Die Architektur des Barock ist sehr aufwendig.
catalogue ['kætəlɔg]	Katalog
I would like to buy the catalogue for that exhibition.	Ich würde gern den Ausstellungskatalog kaufen.
Classicism ['klæsɪsɪzəm]	Klassizismus
Classicism was a movement where the art of ancient Greece was imitated.	Klassizismus war eine Kunstrichtung, in der die Kunst der Antike nachgeahmt wurde.
to create [kriː'eɪt]	schaffen
He has created several beautiful works of art.	Er hat einige wunderschöne Kunstwerke geschaffen.
creation [kriː'eɪʃən]	Schöpfung
He will reveal his new creation tomorrow.	Er wird seine neue Schöpfung morgen enthüllen.
Cubism [kjuːbɪzəm]	Kubismus
Picasso was one of the main Cubist artists.	Picasso war einer der Hauptkünstler des Kubismus.
Dadaism ['dɑːdəɪzəm]	Dadaismus

exhibition [eksɪ'bɪʃən]	Ausstellung
Expressionism [ɪk'spreʃənɪzəm]	Expressionismus
Kandinsky and Kokoschka were representatives of Expressionism.	Kandinsky und Kokoschka waren Repräsentanten des Expressionismus.
fine arts [faɪn ɑːts]	Schöne Künste
There are several schools for the fine arts in New York.	Es gibt in New York einige Schulen für die Schönen Künste.
Gothic ['gɔθɪk]	Gotik
The cathedral is an excellent example of Gothic architecture.	Der Dom ist ein ausgezeichnetes Beispiel gotischer Architektur.
illustration [ɪləs'treɪʃən]	Abbildung
image ['ɪmɪdʒ]	Bild
Impressionism [ɪm'preʃənɪzəm]	Impressionismus
Impressionism started in France.	Der Impressionismus hat seinen Ursprung in Frankreich.
inspiration [ɪnspɪ'reɪʃən]	Inspiration
Gaugin found his inspiration in Tahiti.	Gaugin fand seine Inspiration auf Tahiti.
perspective [pə'spektɪv]	Perspektive
proportion [prə'pɔːʃən]	Proportion
The proportions are distorted.	Die Proportionen sind verzerrt.

to restore [rɪ'stɔː]	restaurieren
They spent years restoring the fresco.	Sie haben Jahre gebraucht, um das Fresko zu restaurieren.
romanesque [rəʊmə'nesk]	romanisch
Romanticism [rəʊ'mæntɪsɪzəm]	Romantik
C. D. Friedrich was a famous Romantic painter.	C. D. Friedrich war ein berühmter Maler der Romantik.
spectrum ['spektrəm]	Spektrum
His work incorporates a broad spectrum of styles.	Sein Werk umfasst ein breites Stilspektrum.
studio ['stjuːdɪəʊ]	Atelier
style [staɪl]	Stil
He paints in the style of the Dadaists.	Er malt im Stil der Dadaisten.
symmetry ['sɪmɪtrɪ]	Symmetrie; Ebenbild
The artists of the Renaissance emphasized symmetry in their work.	Die Künstler der Renaissance betonten die Symmetrie in ihren Werken.
visual ['vɪzjʊəl]	visuell

Art expressions

to see an exhibition: eine Ausstellung besuchen
to draw: zeichnen
to make a sketch: skizzieren
to mix paints: Farben mischen
to visualize: visualisieren

2. Malerei und Grafik

background ['bækgraʊnd]	Hintergrund
The background is too dark.	Der Hintergrund ist zu dunkel.
brush [brʌʃ]	Pinsel
He uses various sized brushes.	Er benutzt Pinsel verschiedener Größen.
box of paints [bɔks əv peɪnts]	Malkasten
canvas ['kænvəs]	Leinwand
That is an enormous canvas.	Das ist eine riesige Leinwand.
caricature ['kærɪkətjʊə]	Karikatur
ceiling fresco ['siːlɪŋ 'freskəʊ]	Deckengemälde
The ceiling fresco in the Sistine Chapel is world famous.	Das Deckengemälde in der Sixtinischen Kapelle ist weltberühmt.
charcoal ['tʃɑːkəʊl]	Zeichenkohle; Kohlestift
drawing ['drɔːɪŋ]	Zeichnung
His early drawings are very crude.	Seine frühen Zeichnungen sind sehr unbedarft.
easel [iːzəl]	Staffelei
The easel is wobbly.	Die Staffelei ist wackelig.
engraving [ɪn'greɪvɪŋ]	Stich
Hogarth did a well-known series of engravings.	Hogarth fertigte eine Reihe von Stichen.

to etch [etʃ]	radieren
etching ['etʃɪŋ]	Radierung
frame [freɪm]	Rahmen
The picture needs a better frame.	Das Bild braucht einen besseren Rahmen.
fresco ['freskəʊ]	Fresko
gallery ['gæləri]	Galerie; Kunsthaus
The gallery is only open in the afternoons or by appointment.	Die Galerie ist nur nachmittags oder nach Vereinbarung geöffnet.
graphic art(s) ['græfik ɑːt(s)]	Grafik
graphic artist ['græfik 'ɑːtɪst]	Grafiker(in)
The agency is looking for a graphic artist.	Die Agentur sucht einen Grafiker.
icon ['aɪkən]	Ikone
There are beautiful icons in old Russian churches.	Es gibt in alten russischen Kirchen schöne Ikonen.
Indian ink ['ɪndɪən ɪŋk]	Tusche
ink [ɪŋk]	Tinte
He signed his name with red ink.	Er unterschrieb mit roter Tinte.
landscape ['lændskeɪp]	Landschaft
Are his landscapes well-known?	Sind seine Landschaftsbilder bekannt?
lithography [lɪ'θəʊgrəfɪ]	Lithografie
mural ['mjʊərəl]	Wandgemälde

The archaeologist found a mural in the tomb.	Der Archäologe entdeckte im Grab ein Wandgemälde.
nude [njuːd]	Akt
He worked as a nude model.	Er arbeitete als Aktmodell.
oil painting [ɔɪl 'peɪntɪŋ]	Ölgemälde
oils [ɔɪlz]	Ölmalerei
old master [əʊld 'mɑːstə]	alter Meister
Titan and Rembrandt are old masters.	Titan und Rembrandt gehören zu den alten Meistern.
paint-brush [peɪnt brʌʃ]	Pinsel
painting ['peɪntiŋ]	Gemälde
palette ['pælət]	Palette
Artists use a palette to mix the colours.	Maler benutzen Paletten, um Farben zu mischen.
parchment ['pɑːtʃmənt]	Pergament
portrait ['pɔːtrɪt]	Porträt
The portrait of her ancestor was done by a famous artist.	Das Porträt ihres Ahnen wurde von einem berühmten Künstler erstellt.
retouching [riː'tʌtʃɪŋ]	Retusche; Übermalung
The photographs will need retouching.	Die Fotos müssen retuschiert werden.
self-portrait [self 'pɔːtrɪt]	Selbstporträt
shading [ʃeɪdiŋ]	Schattierung
to sketch [sketʃ]	skizzieren
He sketched the outline of the building.	Er skizzierte die Umrisse des Gebäudes.

sketch [sketʃ]	Skizze
still-life [stɪl laɪf]	Stillleben
She photographed a still-life composed of automobile parts.	Sie fotografierte ein Stillleben aus Autoteilen.
water-colour ['wɔːtə 'kʌlə]	Aquarell
woodcut ['wʊdkʌt]	Holzschnitt

3. Bildhauerei

art of sculpture [ɑːt əv 'skʌlptʃə]	Bildhauerei
bust [bʌst]	Büste
Did you see the bust of Ceasar?	Hast du die Büste Cäsars gesehen?
cast [kɑːst]	Guss
He made a cast of the statue.	Er machte einen Guss der Statue.
granite ['grænɪt]	Granit
Granite is very hard.	Granit ist sehr hart.
high relief [haɪ rɪ'liːf]	Hochrelief
low relief [ləʊ rɪ'liːf]	Basrelief; Flachrelief
marble ['mɑːbl]	Marmor
The floor is made of marble.	Der Boden ist aus Marmor.
monument ['mɔnjʊmənt]	Denkmal
They erected a monument to those who were killed in the war.	Sie errichteten ein Denkmal für die Gefallenen.

plaster ['plɑːstə]	Gips
The model is made of plaster.	Das Modell ist aus Gips.
sculptor ['skʌlptə]	Bildhauer
Michelangelo was a famous sculptor.	Michelangelo war ein berühmter Bildhauer.
sculptress ['skʌlptrɪs]	Bildhauerin
sculpture ['skʌlptʃə]	Skulptur
"The Thinker" is a sculpture by Rodin.	„Der Denker" ist eine Skulptur von Rodin.

4. Architektur

architecture ['ɑːkɪtektʃə]	Architektur
architrave ['ɑːkɪtreɪv]	Architrav; Tragbalken
bungalow ['bʌŋgələʊ]	Bungalow
column ['kɔləm]	Säule
The building has five columns.	Das Gebäude hat fünf Säulen.

Other words with the silent mn
solemn: feierlich
autumn: Herbst
hymn: Hymne

façade [fə'sɑːd]	Fassade
interior design [ɪn'tiːrɪə dɪ'zaɪn]	Innenausstattung

They hired someone to do the interior design. | Sie haben jemanden mit der Innenausstattung beauftragt.

keystone ['kiːstəʊn] | Schlussstein
The keystone was laid in a special ceremony. | Der Schlussstein wurde in einer speziellen Zeremonie gelegt.

mosaic [məʊ'zeɪɪk] | Mosaik
to rebuild [riː'bɪld] | wieder aufbauen
relief [ri'liːf] | Relief
to renovate ['renəʊveɪt] | renovieren
It took them a year to renovate the old house completely. | Sie haben ein Jahr gebraucht, um das alte Haus komplett zu renovieren.

skyscraper ['skaɪskreɪpə] | Wolkenkratzer
The big city New York has many important skyscrapers. | Die Großstadt New York hat viele bedeutende Wolkenkratzer.
support [sə'pɔːt] | Stütze
terraced house ['terəsd haʊs] | Reihenhaus

Irregular past tense
to hold an exhibition: Lila held an exhibition.
to draw from life: He drew from life.
to sit for a portrait: Marie sat for her portrait.
to think up a concept: She thought up a concept.

Literatur

1. Literatur allgemein und Stil

allegory ['ælɪgərɪ]	Allegorie
alliteration [əlɪtə'reɪʃən]	Alliteration; Stabreim
analogy [ə'nælədʒɪ]	Analogie
author [ɔːθə]	Autor(in)
chapter ['tʃæptə]	Kapitel
The novel has 20 chapters.	Der Roman hat 20 Kapitel.
counterplot ['kaʊntəplɔt]	Gegenhandlung
dedication [dedɪ'keɪʃən]	Widmung
The dedication is to his mother.	Die Widmung gilt seiner Mutter.
description [dɪ'scrɪpʃən]	Beschreibung
Her description of London life is perfect.	Ihre Beschreibung vom Londoner Leben ist perfekt.
dialogue ['daɪəlɔg]	Dialog
The dialogue is a bit unimaginative.	Der Dialog ist etwas einfallslos.

Words with -ogue pronounced as -og
monologue: Monolog
travelogue: Reisebuch
catalogue: Katalog

eloquence ['eləkwens]	Eloquenz

epilogue ['epɪlɒg] — Epilog
The epilogue takes place ten years later. — Der Epilog spielt zehn Jahre später.
foreword ['fɔːwɜːd] — Vorwort
genre ['ʒɑːnrə] — Gattung
The novel does not fit into one specific genre. — Der Roman ist keiner einzelnen Gattung zuzuordnen.
hardback ['hɑːdbæk] — gebundene Ausgabe; fester Einband
They are offering discounts on hardbacks. — Sie bieten Rabatt auf gebundene Ausgaben.
hero ['hiːrəʊ] — Held
The hero turns out to be the villain. — Der Held entpuppt sich als Bösewicht.
humour [hjuːmə] — Humor
A strange sense of humour! — Ein seltsamer Humor!
image ['ɪmɪdʒ] — Bild
irony ['aɪərənɪ] — Ironie
Oscar Wilde was famous for his irony. — Oscar Wilde war für seine Ironie bekannt.
jest [dʒest] — Witz
He said it in jest. — Er hat es als Witz gemeint.
metaphor ['metəfə] — Metapher
motive ['məʊtɪv] — Motiv
paperback ['peɪpəbæk] — Taschenbuch
I bought the paperback edition. — Ich habe die Taschenbuchausgabe gekauft.

pathos ['peɪθɔs]	Pathos
The scene with the dying child is described with great pathos.	Die Szene mit dem sterbenden Kind wird mit großem Pathos beschrieben.
plot [plɔt]	Handlung
The plot is not very logical.	Die Handlung ist nicht sehr schlüssig.
preface ['prefɪs]	Vorwort
He describes the origin of his book in the preface.	Im Vorwort beschreibt er das Entstehen seines Buches.
quote [kwəʊt]	Zitat
Is that quote from Shakespeare?	Ist dieses Zitat von Shakespeare?
realism ['rɪəlɪzəm]	Realismus
trilogy ['trɪlədʒɪ]	Trilogie

2. Prosa

biography [baɪ'ɔgrəfɪ]	Biografie
I am reading a biography of Napoleon.	Ich lese eine Biografie über Napoleon.
declamation [deklə'meɪʃən]	Rede
detective novel [dɪ'tektɪv 'nɔvəl]	Detektivroman
Henning Mankell has written several excellent detective novels.	Henning Mankell hat einige ausgezeichnete Detektivromane geschrieben.

Several famous detective novel authors in the English language
Sir Arthur Conan Doyle: His famous detective was Sherlock Holmes with his partner Dr. Watson.
Agatha Christie: Her two most famous detectives are Hercule Poirot and Miss Jane Marple.
Dashiell Hammet: He writes about the adventures of the detective Phillip Marlowe.

diary ['daɪərɪ]	Tagebuch
Her diary was published after her death.	Ihr Tagebuch wurde nach ihrem Tod veröffentlicht.
fable ['feɪbl]	Fabel
"The Tortoise and the Hare" is a famous fable.	„Der Hase und der Igel" ist eine bekannte Fabel.
fairy tale ['fɛərɪ teɪl]	Märchen
"The Little Mermaid" is a fairy tale.	„Die kleine Meerjungfrau" ist ein Märchen.
fantasy ['fæntəsɪ]	Fantasyroman; märchenhafte Erzählung
fiction ['fɪkʃən]	Unterhaltungsliteratur; Belletristik
She refuses to read fiction.	Sie weigert sich, Belletristik zu lesen.
Gothic Novel ['gɔθɪk 'nɔvəl]	Schauerroman
Gothic novels were popular in the 19th century.	Schauerromane waren im 19. Jahrhundert populär.

historical novel [hɪs'tɔrɪkəl 'nɔvəl]	historischer Roman
"War and Peace" is a historical novel.	„Krieg und Frieden" ist ein historischer Roman.
key novel [kiː 'nɔvəl]	Schlüsselroman
"Wilhelm Meister's Apprenticeship" is one of Goethe's key novels.	„Wilhelm Meisters Lehrjahre" ist einer von Goethes Schlüsselromanen.
legend ['ledʒənd]	Legende
The story of Robin Hood is an English legend.	Die Geschichte von Robin Hood ist eine britische Legende.
memoirs ['memwɑːz]	Memoiren
myth [mɪθ]	Mythos
The ancient Greeks had many myths.	Die Griechen hatten viele Mythen.
narration [nə'reɪʃən]	Erzählung; Schilderung
novel ['nɔvəl]	Roman
oration [ɔː'reɪʃən]	Ansprache
Brutus' oration over the body of Ceasar is a famous Shakespeare speech.	Brutus' Ansprache an die Leiche Cäsars ist eine bekannte Rede von Shakespeare.
paragraph ['pærəgrɑːf]	Absatz
You need to break up the text into paragraphs.	Du musst den Text in Absätze aufteilen.
persona [pɜː'səʊnə]	fiktiver Erzähler
prose [prəʊz]	Prosa

I like his poetry better than his prose.	Mir gefallen seine Gedichte besser als seine Prosa.
pun [pʌn]	Wortspiel
He made a pun on the word "run".	Er erfand ein Wortspiel mit dem Wort „run".
romance [rəʊ'mæns]	Abenteuerroman
saga ['sɑːgə]	Sage; Saga; Geschichtsroman
satire ['sætaɪə]	Satire
short story [ʃɔːt 'stɔːrɪ]	Kurzgeschichte
tale [teɪl]	Erzählung
whodunit [huː'dʌnɪt]	Kriminalroman

3. Dichtung und Schauspiel

act [ækt]	Akt; Aufzug
A classical tragedy has five acts.	Eine klassische Tragödie hat fünf Akte.
anthology [æn'θɔlədʒɪ]	Sammlung
ballad ['bæləd]	Ballade
blank verse [blænk vɜːs]	Blankvers
Blank verse does not rhyme.	Ein Blankvers reimt sich nicht.
burlesque [bɜː'lesk]	Burleske
cadence ['keɪdəns]	Kadenz; Versschluss
The cadence is falling.	Der Versschluss ist abfallend.
comedy ['kɔmədɪ]	Komödie

Neil Simon wrote many comedies.	Neil Simon schrieb viele Komödien.
comic relief ['kɔmɪk rɪ'liːf]	komische Auflösung
drama ['drɑːmə]	Drama
dramatic irony [drə'mætɪk 'aɪrənɪ]	dramatische Ironie
elegy ['elədʒiː]	Elegie
epic ['epɪk]	Epos
"The Niebelungs" is a famous German epic.	„Die Niebelungen" ist ein bekanntes deutsches Epos.
farce [fɑːs]	Farce
foot [fʊt]	Fuß
iamb ['aɪæm]	Jambus
limerick ['lɪmərɪk]	Scherzgedicht; Limerick
lyric ['lɪrɪk]	Lyrik
melodrama ['melədrɑːmə]	Melodrama
meter ['miːtə]	Metrum
metrics ['metrɪks]	Verskunst
nursery rhyme ['nɜːsərɪ raɪm]	Kinderreim

A famous English nursery rhyme

Georgy Porgy pudding pie,
kissed the girls and made them cry,
when the boys came out to play,
Georgy Porgy ran away.

ode [əʊd]	Ode

play [pleɪ]	Theaterstück
We are going to see the new play by Smith.	Wir schauen uns das neue Theaterstück von Smith an.
playwright [pleɪraɪt]	Bühnenautor; Dramatiker
Marlowe was a famous playwright and contemporary of Shakespeare.	Marlowe war ein berühmter Dramatiker und Zeitgenosse Shakespeares.
poetry ['pəʊɪtrɪ]	Dichtung
to recite a poem	ein Gedicht rezitieren
rhapsody ['ræpsədɪ]	Rhapsodie
scene [siːn]	Szene
sonnet ['sɔnɪt]	Sonett
stanza ['stænzə]	Strophe
How many stanzas does a ballad have?	Wie viele Strophen hat eine Ballade?
tragedy ['trædʒədɪ]	Tragödie
"Agamemnon" is a famous Greek tragedy.	„Agamemnon" ist eine berühmte griechische Tragödie.

Mathematik

to add [æd]	addieren
Add the two columns of figures together!	Addiere die zwei Zahlenspalten!
addition [ɔ'dɪʃən]	Addition
algebra ['ældʒɪbrɔ]	Algebra

Algebra uses a combination of letters and numbers.	In der Algebra verwendet man sowohl Zahlen als auch Buchstaben.
angle ['æŋgl]	Winkel
The angle is 90 degrees.	Der Winkel hat 90 Grad.
arithmetics [ə'rɪθmətɪks]	Rechnen
to bisect [baɪ'sekt]	halbieren
Bisect the circle!	Halbiere den Kreis!
calculation [kælkjʊ'leɪʃən]	Rechnung
be out in one's calculation	sich verrechnet haben
circle ['sɜːkəl]	Kreis
cube [kjuːb]	Würfel
decimal ['desɪməl]	dezimal
decipher [dɪ'saɪfə]	entziffern
degree [dɪ'griː]	Grad
denominator [dɪ'nɔmɪneɪtə]	Nenner
diagram ['daɪəgræm]	Diagramm; Schaltbild
to divide [dɪ'vaɪd]	dividieren
9 divided by 3 is 3.	9 dividiert durch 3 ist 3.
division [dɪ'vɪʒən]	Division
equal to ['iːkwəl tuː]	gleich
error ['erə]	Fehler
even ['iːvən]	gerade
2, 4, 6, and 8 are even numbers.	2, 4, 6 und 8 sind gerade Zahlen.
figure ['fɪgə]	Ziffer
graph [grɑːf]	Diagramm
minus ['maɪnəs]	minus

3 minus 2 is 1.	3 minus 2 ist 1.
minus sign ['maɪnəs saɪn]	Minuszeichen
multiplication [mʌltɪplɪ'keɪʃən]	Multiplikation
to multiply ['mʌltɪplaɪ]	multiplizieren
If you multiply 3 by 5 you get 15.	3 multipliziert mit 5 ist 15.
odd [ɔd]	ungerade
1, 3, 5 and 7 are odd numbers.	1, 3, 5 und 7 sind ungerade Zahlen.
parallel ['pærəlel]	parallel
plus [plʌs]	plus
2 plus 2 equals 4.	2 plus 2 ist 4.
plus sign [plʌs saɪn]	Pluszeichen
probability [prɔbə'bɪlɪtɪ]	Wahrscheinlichkeit
Can you calculate the probability?	Kannst du die Wahrscheinlichkeit berechnen?
quarter ['kwɔːtə]	Viertel
rectangle ['rektæŋgl]	Rechteck
scale [skeɪl]	Skala; Maßstab
sign [saɪn]	Vorzeichen
There are two signs: positive and negative.	Es gibt zwei Vorzeichen: plus und minus.
sphere [sfɪə]	Kugel
square [skwɛə]	Viereck
to subtract [səb'trækt]	abziehen
Don't forget to subtract your expenses!	Vergiss nicht, deine Ausgaben abzuziehen!

subtraction [səb'trækʃən]	Subtraktion
sum [sʌm]	Summe
The sum is shown at the bottom.	Die Summe wird unten angezeigt.
triangle ['traɪæŋgl]	Dreieck
verification [verɪfɪ'keɪʃən]	Gegenprobe
x-axis [eks'æksɪs]	x-Achse

Medien

1. Rundfunk und Fernsehen

advertising ['ædvətaɪzɪŋ]	Werbung
They invested a good deal of money in advertising.	Sie haben viel Geld in Werbung investiert.
announcer [ə'naʊnsə]	Ansager(in)
You can hear the announcer's American accent.	Der amerikanische Akzent des Ansagers ist hörbar.
to broadcast ['brɔːdkɑːst]	ausstrahlen
They only broadcast violent films after 10 p.m.	Gewaltfilme werden erst nach 22 Uhr ausgestrahlt.
caption ['kæpʃən]	Untertitel
The program has captions for the deaf.	Die Sendung hat einen Untertitel für Taube.
channel ['tʃænəl]	Kanal
commercial [kə'mɜːʃəl]	Werbespot; Reklamesendung

I saw a funny commercial for beer last night.	Gestern Abend habe ich einen witzigen Werbespot für Bier gesehen.
correspondent ['kɔrɪs'pɔndənt(ɪn)]	Korrespondent(in)
She is the network's Russia correspondent.	Sie ist die Russlandkorrespondentin des Senders.
coverage ['kʌvərɪdʒ]	Berichterstattung
I find the coverage of the election too one-sided.	Ich finde die Berichterstattung über den Wahlkampf zu einseitig.
current affairs ['kʌrənt ə'fɛəz]	Aktuelles
dead air [ded ɛə]	Sendepause
There was half-an-hour of dead air.	Es gab eine halbe Stunde Sendepause.
documentary [dɔkjʊ'mentərɪ]	Dokumentarfilm
I saw an excellent documentary about the Civil War.	Ich habe einen exzellenten Dokumentarfilm über den amerikanischen Bürgerkrieg gesehen.
eyewitness ['aɪwɪtnɪs]	Augenzeuge; Augenzeugin
They interviewed eyewitnesses at the scene of the crime.	Sie interviewten Augenzeugen am Tatort.
feature ['fiːtʃə]	Reportage; Sonderbericht
to inform [ɪn'fɔːm]	informieren

She is trying to get some information before deciding. — Sie versucht sich zu informieren, bevor sie eine Entscheidung trifft.

interview ['ɪntəvjuː] — Interview; Befragung

live broadcast [laɪv 'brɔːdkɑːst] — Direktübertragung

The opera will be a live broadcast from the Vienna State Opera. — Die Oper wird eine Direktübertragung aus der Wiener Staatsoper sein.

moderator ['mɔdəreɪtə] — Diskussionsleiter(in)

I thought the moderator was too aggressive. — Ich fand den Diskussionsleiter zu agressiv.

network ['netwɜːk] — Sendernetz

news [njuːz] — Nachrichten

John watches the news every night at eight. — John schaut jeden Abend um 20 Uhr Nachrichten.

news bulletin [njuːz 'bʊlətɪn] — Meldung

A news bulletin has just come in from Brazil. — Gerade ist eine Meldung aus Brasilien eingetroffen.

news report [njuːz rɪ'pɔːt] — Nachrichtensendung

news broadcast ['njuːz'brɔːdkɑːst] — Nachrichtensendung

newsreader ['njuːzriːdə] — Nachrichtensprecher(in)

poll [pəʊl] — Umfrage

The poll shows that most citizens trust their Members of Parliament. — Die Umfrage zeigt, dass die meisten Bürger ihren Ministern vertrauen.

programme ['prəʊgræm]	Programm
public ['pʌblɪk]	Öffentlichkeit; öffentlich
I can't believe he did that in public!	Ich kann nicht glauben, dass er das in der Öffentlichkeit getan hat!
He only watches public television.	Er schaut nur öffentlich-rechtliches Fernsehen.
public relations (PR) ['pʌblɪk rɪ'leɪʃənz]	Öffentlichkeitsarbeit
He has invested a great deal of money in public relations.	Er hat viel Geld in Öffentlichkeitsarbeit investiert.
radio ['reɪdɪəʊ]	Rundfunk; Radio
radio play ['reɪdɪəʊ pleɪ]	Hörspiel
report [rɪ'pɔːt]	Bericht; Reportage
We saw a report about child labour last night.	Gestern Abend haben wir einen Bericht über Kinderarbeit gesehen.
reporter [rɪ'pɔːtə]	Berichterstatter(in)
script [skrɪpt]	Drehbuch
Her script was accepted by the producer.	Der Produzent hat ihr Drehbuch angenommen.
scriptwriter ['skrɪptraɪtə]	Drehbuchautor(in)
She worked as a scriptwriter for TV movies.	Sie arbeitete als Drehbuchautorin für Fernsehfilme.
serial ['sɪərɪəl]	Sendereihe
source [sɔːs]	Quelle
He refuses to name his source.	Er weigert sich, seine Quelle zu nennen.

sponsor ['spɔnsə]	Förderer; Förderin
The show is sponsored by the telephone company.	Die Sendung wird von der Telefongesellschaft gefördert.
talk show [tɔːk ʃəʊ]	Diskussionsrunde
The talk show was very lively.	Die Diskussionsrunde war sehr lebhaft.
television ['telɪvɪʒən]	Fernsehen; Fernseher
topic ['tɔpɪk]	Thema
The topic is the growing rate of unemployment.	Das Thema ist die zunehmende Arbeitslosigkeit.
topical ['tɔpɪkəl]	aktuell
to transmit [trænz'mɪt]	senden
They are transmitting simultaneously from two locations.	Sie senden von zwei verschiedenen Orten gleichzeitig.
video ['vɪdɪəʊ]	Video
weather report ['weðə rɪ'pɔːt]	Wetterbericht
The weather report forecast rain.	Der Wetterbericht sagt Regen voraus.

2. Zeitungen, Zeitschriften und Verlag

advertisement [əd'vɜːtɪsmənt]	Anzeige; Inserat
We met through an advertisement.	Wir haben uns über eine Anzeige kennen gelernt.

article ['ɑːtɪkl]	Artikel; Beitrag
She wrote an article about the new exhibition.	Sie hat einen Artikel über die neue Ausstellung geschrieben.
by-line ['baɪlaɪn]	Verfasserangabe
caption ['kæpʃən]	Titel; Überschrift; Bildunterschrift
The caption is very witty.	Die Überschrift ist sehr geistreich.
censorship ['sensəʃɪp]	Zensur
circulation [sɜːkjʊ'leɪʃən]	Auflage
The paper has a circulation of 200,000.	Die Zeitung hat eine Auflage von 200.000.
clipping ['klɪpɪŋ]	Zeitungsausschnitt
compositor [kəm'pɔzɪtə]	Schriftsetzer(in)
The compositor said the article would not fit on one page.	Der Schriftsetzter meinte, dass der Artikel nicht auf eine Seite passen würde.
contribution [kɔntrɪ'bjuːʃən]	redaktioneller Beitrag
He makes one contribution a week.	Er schreibt pro Woche einen redaktionellen Beitrag.
copy ['kɔpɪ]	Ausgabe; Exemplar
I would like three copies.	Ich hätte gern drei Exemplare.
copyright ['kɔpɪraɪt]	Urheberrecht
Did you check the copyright on that picture?	Hast du das Urheberrecht dieses Bildes überprüft?

cover ['kʌvə] — Titelblatt
Her face was on the cover of three fashion magazines. — Ihr Gesicht war auf dem Titelblatt von drei Modezeitschriften.

critic ['krɪtɪk] — Kritiker(in)
The critics seem to hate the new play. — Die Kritiker scheinen das neue Theaterstück zu hassen.

daily ['deɪlɪ] — Tageszeitung
The New York Times is a daily. — Die New York Times ist eine Tageszeitung.
to edit ['edɪt] — herausgeben; redigieren
edition [ɪ'dɪʃən] — Ausgabe
She read it in the evening edition. — Sie hat es in der Abendausgabe gelesen.
pocket edition — Taschenbuchausgabe
editor ['edɪtə] — Redakteur(in)
The editor rejected his article. — Der Redakteur hat seinen Artikel abgelehnt.
editorial [edɪ'tɔːrɪəl] — Leitartikel
foreign press ['fɔrən pres] — Auslandspresse
gazette [gə'zet] — Zeitung
gossip column ['gɔsɪp 'kɔləm] — Klatschspalte
The gossip columns have been saying that they are together. — Die Klatschspalten munkeln, dass sie ein Paar sind.
illustration [ɪlə'streɪʃən] — Abbildung

imprint ['ɪmprɪnt]	Impressum
journal ['dʒɜːnl]	Journal; Blatt
He reads the medical journals every week.	Er liest die medizinischen Fachzeitschriften jede Woche.
journalist ['dʒɜːnəlɪst]	Journalist(in)
lead story [liːd 'stɔːrɪ]	Hauptartikel
magazine [mægə'ziːn]	Zeitschrift
She loves to read auto magazines.	Sie liest sehr gerne Automobilzeitschriften.
news agency [njuːz 'eɪdʒənsɪ]	Nachrichtenagentur
X is a well-known news agency.	X ist eine bekannte Nachrichtenagentur.
news item [njuːz 'aɪtəm]	Zeitungsnotiz
number ['nʌmbə]	Ausgabe
opinion leader [ə'pɪnjən 'liːdə]	Meinungsmacher
Well-known journalists often act as opinion leaders.	Bekannte Journalisten wirken oft als Meinungsmacher.

False Friends

Watch out!

Meinung cannot be translated into *meaning*. *Meaning* in German is *Bedeutung*.

Ex: I don't understand the meaning.

Ich verstehe die Bedeutung nicht.

page [peɪdʒ]	Seite
The editorial is on page two.	Der Leitartikel steht auf Seite zwei.
pamphlet ['pæmflɪt]	Flugblatt; Prospekt
The Union of Socialist Students were distributing pamphlets.	Der Verein sozialistischer Studenten verteilte Flugblätter.
paper war ['peɪpə wɔː]	Pressepolemik
Her comment started a paper war.	Ihr Kommentar führte zu Pressepolemik.
periodical [pɪərɪ'ɔdɪkl]	Zeitschrift
The library has a periodical section.	Die Bibliothek hat eine Zeitschriftenabteilung.
picture editor ['pɪktʃə 'edɪtə]	Bildredakteur(in)
The picture editor found the photo too gory.	Der Bildredakteur hielt das Bild für zu brutal.
polemic [pə'lemɪk]	Streitschrift
press [pres]	Presse
The press responded in different ways.	Die Presse reagierte auf verschiedene Weise.
press agency [pres 'eɪdʒənsɪ]	Presseagentur
press conference [pres 'kɔnfərəns]	Pressekonferenz
The company announced its bankruptcy at a press conference.	Die Firma gab ihre Insolvenz in einer Pressekonferenz bekannt.

print [prɪnt]	Druck

Parts of an article
headline: Überschrift; Schlagzeile
copy: Fließtext
sub-headline: Untertitel
caption: Bildunterschrift

printing error ['prɪntɪŋ 'erə]	Druckfehler
proof [pruːf]	Probeabzug; Fahne
The agency always sends two proofs.	Die Agentur schickt immer zwei Fahnen.
publication [pʌblɪ'keɪʃən]	Veröffentlichung
The publishing group has several publications about psychology.	Die Verlagsgruppe vertreibt einige Veröffentlichungen über Psychologie.
publicist ['pʌblɪsɪst]	Publizist(in)
to publish ['pʌblɪʃ]	veröffentlichen; herausgeben; verlegen
She published three books in three years.	Sie brachte drei Bücher in drei Jahren heraus.
publishing house ['pʌblɪʃɪŋ haʊs]	Verlag
readership ['riːdəʃɪp]	Leserschaft
The paper's readership is declining.	Die Leserschaft der Zeitung nimmt ab.
regional press ['riːdʒənəl pres]	Regionalpresse

The regional press provides more in-depth coverage of local news.	Die Regionalpresse bietet eine ausführlichere Berichterstattung über lokale Nachrichten.
reprint ['riːprɪnt]	Nachdruck
to retouch [riː'tʌtʃ]	retuschieren
The photographer retouched the picture to make Dean look younger.	Der Fotograf retuschierte das Bild, um Dean jünger aussehen zu lassen.
review [rɪ'vjuː]	Rezension
There is a review of the new book in today's paper.	Es gibt in der heutigen Zeitung eine Rezension des neuen Buchs.
to rewrite [riː'raɪt]	umformulieren
royalties ['rɔɪəltiːz]	Autorenhonorar; Tantimien
Her last book was so successful that she can live from the royalties.	Ihr letztes Buch war so erfolgreich, dass sie vom Honorar leben kann.
run [rʌn]	Druckgang
scoop [skuːp]	Knüller
His supposed scoop turned out to be a rumour.	Sein vermeintlicher Knüller entpuppte sich als Gerücht.
special edition ['speʃəl ɪ'dɪʃən]	Sonderausgabe
specimen ['spesɪmɪn]	Ansichtsexemplar
Could you send me a specimen of your paper?	Könnten Sie mir ein Ansichtsexemplar Ihrer Zeitung zukommen lassen?

stop press [stɔp pres]	letzte Mitteilungen
story ['stɔːrɪ]	Artikel
Did you read the story about the child armies?	Hast Du den Artikel über Kinderarmeen gelesen?
sub-editor ['sʌbedɪtə]	Redakteur(in); zweiter Schriftleiter
She worked as a sub-editor for two years before becoming editor-in-chief.	Sie arbeitete zwei Jahre als Redakteurin, bevor sie Chefredakteurin wurde.
sub-editing ['sʌbedɪtɪŋ]	Redigieren eines Textes
subscribe ['səbskraɪb]	abonnieren
He subscribes to two dailies.	Er abonniert zwei Tageszeitungen.
supplement ['sʌpləmənt]	Beilage
Have you seen the weekend supplement?	Hast du die Wochenendbeilage gesehen?
tabloid ['tæblɔɪd]	Sensationsblatt
title page ['taɪtl peɪdʒ]	Titelseite
The picture of the royal family is on the title page.	Das Foto der Königsfamilie ist auf der Titelseite.
yellow press ['jeləʊ pres]	Sensations-, Boulevardpresse

3. Fotografie, Filmen und Kino

distribution [dɪstrɪ'bjuːʃən]	Filmverleih
The film will only be distributed to art-house cinemas.	Der Film wird nur an Kunstkinos verliehen.

photograph ['fəʊtəgrɑːf] — Foto
photographer [fə'tɒgrəfə] — Fotograf(in)
The photographer was shot in the war zone. — Der Fotograf wurde im Kriegsgebiet erschossen.
poster ['pəʊstə] — Plakat
print [prɪnt] — Abzug
Can you make me another set of prints? — Kannst du mir weitere Abzüge machen?
screen [skriːn] — Leinwand
The screen in this cinema is too small. — Die Leinwand in diesem Kino ist zu klein.
to shoot [ʃuːt] — filmen
They shot the scene in three days. — Sie haben die Szene in drei Tagen gefilmt.
sound effects [saʊnd ɪ'fekts] — Geräuscheffekte

Mensch und Medizin

1. Mensch

abdomen ['æbdəmen] — Unterleib
She awoke with a pain in her abdomen. — Sie wachte mit Unterleibsschmerzen auf.
adolescence [ædə'lesns] — Jugend(zeit); Pubertät
Adolescence is not an easy time. — Die Pubertät ist eine schwierige Zeit.

anatomy [ə'nætəmɪ]	Anatomie
Medical students learn anatomy in their first year.	Medizinstudenten lernen im ersten Jahr Anatomie.
ankle ['ænkl]	Fußknöchel
Her ankle was sore.	Ihr Fußknöchel war empfindlich.
anxiety [æŋ'zaɪətɪ]	Angstzustände; Nervosität
He suffered from anxiety for several years.	Er litt einige Jahre unter Angstzuständen.
appendix [ə'pendɪks]	Blinddarm
She has to have her appendix out.	Ihr Blinddarm muss entfernt werden.
apprehension [æprɪ'henʃn]	Besorgnis
I am apprehensive about the results.	Ich bin wegen der Ergebnisse besorgt.
artery ['ɑːtərɪ]	Ader
blood [blʌd]	Blut
Have you ever donated blood?	Hast du je Blut gespendet?
blood pressure [blʌd 'preʃə]	Blutdruck
He suffers from high blood pressure.	Er hat einen hohen Blutdruck.
bowels ['baʊəlz]	Eingeweide
chest [tʃest]	Brustkorb
childhood ['tʃaɪldhʊd]	Kindheit
We had a nice childhood.	Wir hatten eine schöne Kindheit.
chromosome ['krəʊməzəʊm]	Chromosom

Every sperm carries two chromosomes.	Jedes Spermium trägt zwei Chromosomen in sich.
circulation [sɜːkjʊ'leɪʃən]	Durchblutung; Kreislauf
Cold hands are a sign of poor circulation.	Kalte Hände sind ein Zeichen von schlechter Durchblutung.
conceited ['kənsiːtəd]	eingebildet
He is so conceited! He thinks every woman is after him.	Er ist so eingebildet! Er denkt, dass jede Frau etwas von ihm will.

ie or ei

There is a rhyme to remember when to write *ie* and when to write *ei*: It goes *i* before *e*, except after *c*, or when sounded like *a* as in weigh.
Ex:
acheive; ceiling (*ei* because after *c*)
believe (*ie* because not after a *c*)
sleigh (*ei* sounds like *a*)

conscientious [kɔnʃɪ'enʃəs]	gewissenhaft
depressed [dɪ'prest]	deprimiert
to digest [daɪ'dʒest]	verdauen
I have problems digesting rich food.	Ich habe Probleme, schweres Essen zu verdauen.
embryo ['embrɪəʊ]	Embryo
emotion [ɪ'məʊʃən]	Emotion
Anne shows emotion.	Anne zeigt Emotionen.

emotional [ɪ'məʊʃənəl]	emotional
Sometimes he gets very emotional.	Manchmal wird er sehr emotional.
enzyme ['enzaɪm]	Enzym
to excrete [ɪk'skriːt]	ausscheiden
When you sweat, you excrete bacteria too.	Wenn du schwitzt, scheidest du auch Bakterien aus.
exhausted [ig'zɔːstɪd]	erschöpft
The parents were exhausted after the long drive.	Die Eltern waren nach der langen Fahrt erschöpft.
extroverted ['ekstrəʊvɜːtɪd]	extrovertiert
She is so extroverted. She'll talk to anyone!	Sie ist so extrovertiert. Sie spricht mit jedem!
eyeball ['aɪbɔːl]	Augapfel
fatigue [fə'tiːg]	Ermüdung
He can run for kilometres and feel no fatigue.	Er kann kilometerlang laufen und spürt überhaupt keine Ermüdung.
foetus ['fiːtəs]	Fötus
The foetus seems to be developing normally.	Der Fötus scheint sich normal zu entwickeln.
introverted ['ɪntrəʊvɜːtɪd]	introvertiert
jaw [dʒɔː]	Kiefer
His jaw has been bothering him.	Sein Kiefer bereitet ihm zurzeit Schmerzen.
jealous ['dʒeləs]	eifersüchtig
He is jealous of every man that comes near her.	Er ist eifersüchtig auf jeden Mann, der ihr nahe kommt.

False Friends

Watch out!
Jealousy (Eifersucht) and *Jalousie* are not the same thing.
Jalousie translated into English is *blind* or *shade*.
Ex: They have pulled down the blinds.
Sie haben die Jalousien heruntergezogen.

joint [dʒɔɪnt]	Gelenk
My joints ache.	Mir schmerzen die Gelenke.
kidney ['kɪdnɪ]	Nieren
kidney machine	künstliche Niere
knee [niː]	Knie
She skinned her knee by falling off her bicycle.	Sie hat sich ihr Knie aufgeschürft, als sie vom Fahrrad fiel.
lonely ['ləʊnlɪ]	einsam
She has been very lonely since her husband died.	Seit dem Tod ihres Mannes ist sie sehr einsam.
loving ['lʌvɪŋ]	liebevoll
She was always a loving daughter.	Sie war immer eine liebevolle Tochter.
muscle ['mʌsl]	Muskel
Her muscles were tense.	Ihre Muskeln waren angespannt.
nerves [nɜːvz]	Nerven
That's just a question of nerves.	Das ist reine Nervensache.

Body part idioms

to be easy on the eyes: schön sein
to have a big mouth: eine große Klappe haben
to have two left feet: ungeschickt sein
to have a sharp tongue: sehr kritisch sein
to foot the bill: die Rechnung übernehmen
to get something off one's chest: etwas loswerden
to cost an arm and a leg: sehr teuer sein
to prick up one's ears: aufmerksam werden
to leg it: schnell weglaufen
to get cold feet: kalte Füße bekommen, Bedenken haben
to do something with a flick of a wrist: etwas ohne Schwierigkeiten machen

nose [nəʊz]	Nase
She has a nose-ring.	Sie hat ein Piercing in der Nase.
old age [əʊld eɪdʒ]	Alter
She is getting forgetful in her old age.	Sie wird im Alter sehr vergesslich.
oral ['ɔːrəl]	Mund-
Good oral hygiene is important.	Gute Mundhygiene ist wichtig.
panic ['pænɪk]	Panik
She panicked when she saw the letter.	Sie ist in Panik geraten, als sie den Brief sah.
pelvis ['pelvɪs]	Becken

Elvis Presley was called *Elvis the Pelvis* because he was the first popular singer to swivel and swing his hips.

placenta [plə'sentə]	Plazenta; Mutterkuchen
pore [pɔː]	Pore
She has large pores.	Sie hat große Poren.
pulse [pʌls]	Puls
His pulse was racing as he opened the door.	Sein Puls raste, als er die Tür öffnete.
rib [rɪb]	Rippe
self-confident [self 'kɔnfɪdənt]	selbstsicher
He is self-confident without being arrogant.	Er ist selbstsicher ohne arrogant zu sein.
shoulder ['ʃəʊldə]	Schulter
The workers are standing shoulder to shoulder.	Die Arbeiter stehen Schulter an Schulter.
skull [skʌl]	Schädel
They found a skull in the backyard.	Sie haben einen Schädel im Garten entdeckt.
sperm [spɜːm]	Spermium; Sperma
spontaneous [spɔn'teɪnɪəs]	spontan
We decided spontaneously to drive to New York.	Wir haben uns spontan entschieden, nach New York zu fahren.
stomach ['stʌmək]	Magen
All of the children had a stomach virus.	Alle Kinder hatten einen Magen-Darm-Virus.

superficial [suːpə'fɪʃəl]	oberflächlich
She is not a good friend because she is so superficial.	Sie ist keine gute Freundin, da sie so oberflächlich ist.
sweat [swet]	Schweiß
Sweat trickled down the back of her neck as she waited for the results.	Schweiß rannte über ihren Nacken, als sie auf die Ergebnisse wartete.
test-tube baby [test tjuːb beɪbɪ]	Retortenbaby
tongue [tʌŋ]	Zunge
The swollen tongue indicates severe poisoning.	Die angeschwollene Zunge deutet auf eine schwere Vergiftung hin.
tonsils ['tɔnsls]	Mandeln
The child needs to have his tonsils out soon.	Die Mandeln des Kindes müssen bald entfernt werden.
urine ['jʊərɪn]	Urin; Harn
The company conducts urine tests to see if their employees are using drugs.	Die Firma führt Urinproben durch, um festzustellen, ob ihre Mitarbeiter Drogen nehmen.
vascular system ['væskjʊlə 'sɪstəm]	Gefäßsystem
wrist [rɪst]	Handgelenk
He sprained his wrist playing tennis.	Er verrenkte sich sein Handgelenk beim Tennisspielen.

2. Gesundheit und Krankheit

abnormality [æbnɔːˈmæːlɪtɪ] — Abnormalität; Anormalität
The lab results indicate an abnormality. — Die Testergebnisse weisen auf eine Abnormalität hin.
abortion [əˈbɔːʃən] — Abtreibung
abscess [ˈæbses] — Geschwür
He is having the abscess on his back treated. — Er lässt das Geschwür auf seinem Rücken behandeln.
to ache [eɪk] — schmerzen
My ear aches. — Mein Ohr schmerzt.

Aches and pains

cold: Schnupfen
nausea: Übelkeit
sinus infection: Nebenhöhlenentzündung
heartburn: Sodbrennen
hernia: Leistenbruch
headache: Kopfschmerzen
to have difficulty breathing: Atembeschwerden haben
chills: Schüttelfrost
fever: Fieber
sore muscles: Muskelkater
ulcer: Magengeschwür
side-cramp: Seitenstich
cough: Husten
hiccups: Schluckauf

acupuncture [ˈækjʊpʌŋktʃə] — Akupunktur
addiction [əˈdɪkʃən] — Sucht
It took many years for him to overcome his heroin addiction. — Es hat einige Jahre gedauert, bis er seine Heroinsucht überwunden hat.
AIDS [eɪdz] — Aids

ailment ['eɪlmənt]	Gebrechen; Leiden
alcoholism ['ælkəhɔlɪzəm]	Alkoholismus
allergy ['ælədʒɪ]	Allergie
She's allergic to milk.	Sie hat eine Milchallergie.
ambulance ['æmbjʊləns]	Krankenwagen
Two ambulances arrived at the house.	Zwei Krankenwagen sind angekommen.
to amputate ['æmpjʊteɪt]	amputieren
His leg had to be amputated, as the cancer had spread.	Sein Bein musste amputiert werden, da der Krebs sich ausgebreitet hatte.
anaesthesia [ænɪs'θiːzɪə]	Anästhesie; Betäubung
The operation requires only a local anaesthesia.	Die Operation erfordert nur eine örtliche Betäubung.
antibiotic [æntɪbaɪ'ɔtɪk]	Antibiotikum
It is possible to cure the infection without taking antibiotics immediately.	Es ist möglich, die Entzündung zu heilen, ohne sofort Antibiotika einzunehmen.
antibodies ['æntibɔdɪz]	Abwehrstoffe; Antikörper
appendicitis [əpendɪ'saɪtɪs]	Blinddarmentzündung
They suspect the pain in her side is appendicitis.	Sie vermuten, dass die Schmerzen auf eine Blinddarmentzündung zurückzuführen sind.
aspirin ['æsprɪn]	Aspirin
asthma ['æsmə]	Asthma

She had asthma as a child, but it improved in adulthood. — Als Kind hatte sie Asthma, aber es ist besser geworden, je älter sie wurde.

autopsy ['ɔːtɔpsɪ] — Autopsie

The autopsy showed that he had been murdered. — Die Autopsie zeigte, dass er ermordet worden war.

bacillus [bə'sɪləs] — Bazillus

back-ache ['bækeɪk] — Rückenschmerzen

I get back-ache when my back gets cold. — Ich bekomme Rückenschmerzen, wenn mein Rücken unterkühlt wird.

bacteria [bæk'tɪərɪə] — Bakterien

bandage ['bændɪdʒ] — Verband; Bandage; Binde

The bandage needs to be changed every other day. — Der Verband muss jeden zweiten Tag gewechselt werden.

benign [bɪ'naɪn] — gutartig

The tumour turned out to be benign. — Der Tumor war nun doch gutartig.

birthcontrol pill [bɜːθkən'trəʊl pɪl] — Antibabypille

She forgot to take her birthcontrol pill regularly and became pregnant. — Sie hat vergessen, die Pille regelmäßig zu nehmen und ist schwanger geworden.

to bleed [bliːd] — bluten

The cut began to bleed profusely. — Die Schnittwunde fing an, heftig zu bluten.

blind [blaɪnd]	blind
blood sugar [blʌd 'ʃʊgə]	Blutzucker
blood test [blʌd test]	Blutprobe; Blutuntersuchung
The blood test showed no sign of infection.	Die Blutprobe zeigte keinen Hinweis auf eine Entzündung.
bodily ['bɔdɪlɪ]	körperlich
bronchitis [brɔŋ'kaɪtɪs]	Bronchitis
to bruise [bruːz]	quetschen
bruise [bruːz]	Bluterguss; Prellung
She had a huge bruise on her knee from her fall.	Sie hatte von ihrem Sturz eine riesige Prellung am Knie.
burn [bɜːn]	Brandwunde; Verbrennung
She ran cold water on the burn.	Sie ließ kaltes Wasser über die Brandwunde fließen.
cancer ['kænsə]	Krebs
cardiology [kɑːdɪ'ɔlədʒɪ]	Kardiologie
cavity [kævɪtɪ]	(Zahn)Loch
Brushing your teeth regularly helps prevent cavities.	Regelmäßiges Zähneputzen schützt vor Löchern.
casualty ['kæʒjʊltɪ]	Unfallstation
catheter ['kæθɪtə]	Katheter
to champ [tʃæmp]	kauen; schmatzen
chemist's ['kemists]	Apotheke
She went to the chemist's to get some aspirin.	Sie ging zur Apotheke, um Aspirin zu holen.

Chemist/drugstore

In British English, the *Apotheke* is known as the *chemist* or the *pharmacist*. These stores resemble the German *Apotheke* in that only prescription drugs and health-related items can be purchased here. In the United States, one goes to the *drug store*. In these stores, prescription drugs can be obtained at the *pharmacy*, a special department. Otherwise, items such as aspirin or herbal medicines can be obtained over the counter, i. e. without a prescription. Along with medicines and health-related items, many of these stores also sell magazines, chewing gum, film etc. *Drug stores* are actually a combination of the German *Apotheke* and *Drogerie*!

chemotherapy [kiːməʊ'θerəpɪ]	Chemotherapie
The latest chemotherapy has really weakened her.	Die letzte Chemotherapie hat sie sehr geschwächt.
chicken-pox ['tʃɪkənpɔks]	Windpocken
If you get chicken-pox once, you usually never get it again.	Hast du einmal Windpocken gehabt, wirst du sie nie wieder bekommen.
cholera ['kɔlərə]	Cholera
A cholera epidemic is raging in the village.	Eine Cholera-Epidemie breitet sich gerade rasch im Dorf aus.
choleric ['kɔlərɪk]	cholerisch
cholesterol [kɔ'lestərəl]	Cholesterin

His cholesterol level is too high.	Sein Cholesterinspiegel ist zu hoch.
cold [kəʊld]	Erkältung
I have had a cold for two weeks now.	Ich bin seit zwei Wochen erkältet.
complaint [kəm'pleɪnt]	Leiden
constipation [kɔnstɪ'peɪʃən]	Verstopfung
to consult [kən'sʌlt]	zu Rate ziehen (Arzt)
She consulted some of the best doctors about her throat.	Sie zog wegen ihres Halses einige der besten Ärzte zu Rate.
contagious [kən'teɪdʒəs]	ansteckend
Is that disease contagious?	Ist diese Krankheit ansteckend?
contra-indication ['kɔntrə ɪndɪ'keɪʃən]	Gegenanzeige
contraceptive [kɔntrə'septɪv]	Verhütungsmittel

Different types of contraceptives

condom: Kondom
diaphragm: Diaphragma
spermicide: Spermizid
IUD: Spirale
birth controll pill: Antibabypille

cough [kɔf]	Husten
His cough comes from heavy smoking.	Sein Husten kommt vom starken Rauchen.
cough mixture [kɔf 'mɪkstʃə]	Hustensaft

cramp [kræmp]	Krampf
to cut [kʌt]	schneiden; eingreifen
I cut my finger while preparing dinner.	Ich habe mich beim Vorbereiten des Abendessens in den Finger geschnitten.
cut [kʌt]	Schnittwunde
cyst [sɪst]	Zyste
She had a cyst in her ovary.	Sie hatte eine Zyste in ihrem Eierstock.
deaf [def]	gehörlos; taub
deficiency [dɪ'fɪʃənsɪ]	Mangel
She suffers from an iron deficiency.	Sie leidet unter Eisenmangel.
delivery [dɪ'lɪvərɪ]	Entbindung
The delivery was very hard.	Die Entbindung war sehr schwer.
dermatologist [dɜːmə'tɔlədʒɪst]	Dermatologe; Dermatologin; Hautarzt; Hautärztin
My dermatologist recommends this lotion.	Mein Hautarzt empfiehlt diese Krem.
diabetic [daɪ'betɪk]	zuckerkrank
Due to his unhealthy diet, he became a diabetic in later life.	Wegen seiner ungesunden Essgewohnheiten ist er später an Zucker erkrankt.
disability [dɪsə'bɪlɪtɪ]	Behinderung
Her disability has never stopped her.	Ihre Behinderung hat ihr nie im Weg gestanden.

disease [dɪ'ziːz]	Erkrankung; Krankheit
The disease is incurable.	Die Krankheit ist unheilbar.
dizziness ['dɪzɪnɪs]	Schwindel
epidemic [epɪ'demɪk]	Epidemie; Seuche
The flu epidemic at the beginning of the 20th century killed many people.	Die Grippeepidemie am Anfang des 20. Jahrhunderts kostete viele Menschenleben.
examination [ɪg'zæmɪ'neɪʃən]	Untersuchung
to faint [feɪnt]	in Ohnmacht fallen
She hadn't eaten all day and fainted in the subway.	Sie hatte den ganzen Tag nichts gegessen und ist in der U-Bahn ohnmächtig geworden.
findings ['faɪndɪŋz]	Befund
fit [fɪt]	Anfall
He hasn't had a fit in three months.	Er hat seit drei Monaten keinen Anfall gehabt.
flatulence ['flætjʊləns]	Blähungen
fracture ['fræktʃə]	Bruch; Fraktur
The X-rays showed the fracture.	Die Röntgenaufnahmen zeigten die Fraktur.
gallstone ['gɔːlstəʊn]	Gallenstein
gynaecologist [gaɪnɪ'kɔlədʒɪst]	Frauenarzt; Frauenärztin
Her gynaecologist conducted the pregnancy test.	Ihr Frauenarzt führte den Schwangerschaftstest durch.

haemorrhoids ['hemərɔɪdz]	Hämorriden
hay fever ['heɪfiːvə]	Heuschnupfen
Her hay fever is really bad in the spring.	Ihr Heuschnupfen ist im Frühling sehr schlimm.
to heal [hiːl]	heilen
The broken bone is healing nicely.	Der Knochenbruch heilt sehr gut.
homeopathy [həʊmɪ'ɔpəθɪ]	Homöopathie
I'm going to try homeopathic medicine for my stomach.	Ich werde ein homöopathisches Mittel für meinen Magen ausprobieren.
immune [ɪ'mjuːn]	immun
Some people are immune to the HIV virus.	Manche Menschen sind gegen den HIV-Virus immun.
impotent ['ɪmpətənt]	impotent
incubator ['ɪnkjuːbeɪtə]	Brutkasten
The premature baby was placed in an incubator.	Die Frühgeburt wurde in einen Brutkasten gelegt.
indigestion [ɪndɪ'dʒestʃən]	Sodbrennen
to infect [ɪn'fekt]	anstecken

Instead of using *infect*, you can also use the verb *give* when talking about illnesses.
Ex: She gave me her cold.
Sie steckte mich mit ihrer Erkältung an.

infection [ɪn'fekʃən]	Infektion; Entzündung

She has a middle-ear infection.	Sie hat eine Mittelohrentzündung.
infectious [ɪn'fekʃəs]	ansteckend; übertragbar
The illness is not infectious for humans.	Die Krankheit ist nicht auf Menschen übertragbar.
infectious diseases [ɪn'fekʃəs dɪ'ziːzəz]	Infektionskrankheiten
inflammation [ɪnflə'meɪʃən]	Entzündung

Pain killers

Here are some names for different types of medicines that ease pain:
anti-inflammatory: entzündungshemmendes Mittel
pain reliever: Schmerzmittel
antihistamine: Antihistamine
sleeping aid: Schlafmittel

influenza [ɪnflʊ'enzə]	Grippe
injection [ɪn'dʒekʃən]	Injektion; Spritze
Anna gives herself insulin injections.	Anna spritzt sich selbst Insulin.
insane [ɪn'seɪn]	verrückt
He has been declared insane.	Er ist für verrückt erklärt worden.
to itch ['ɪtʃ]	jucken
The mosquito bite really itches.	Der Mückenstich juckt sehr.
labour ['leɪbə]	Entbindung

labour pains ['leɪbə peɪns] — Wehen
The labour pains set in about two hours ago. — Die Wehen haben vor zwei Stunden eingesetzt.
laxative ['læksətɪv] — Abführmittel
He took a laxative for his constipation but it didn't help. — Er nahm ein Abführmittel gegen seine Verstopfung, aber es hat nicht geholfen.
leukaemia ['luː'kiːmɪə] — Leukämie
Leukaemia affects the white blood cells. — Leukämie greift die weißen Blutkörperchen an.
lumbago [lʌm'beɪgəʊ] — Hexenschuss
lump [lʌmp] — Knoten
The doctor found a lump in her breast. — Der Arzt entdeckte einen Knoten in ihrer Brust.
lying-in ['laɪɪŋ ɪn] — Wochenbett
malignant [mə'lɪgnənt] — bösartig
The lump turned out to be a malignant tumour. — Der Knoten war ein bösartiger Tumor.
measles ['miːzlz] — Masern
There is a vaccination against measles. — Es gibt eine Impfung gegen Masern.
medicine ['medsɪn] — Heilkunde; Medizin; Heilmittel
mentally ill ['mentəlɪ ɪl] — geisteskrank
menopause ['menəʊpɔːz] — Wechseljahre
She is 50 and hasn't been through menopause yet. — Sie ist 50 und ist noch nicht in die Wechseljahre gekommen.

mental illness ['mentl'ɪlnɪs]	Geisteskrankheit
Schizophrenia is a mental illness.	Schizophrenie ist eine Geisteskrankheit.
migraine ['mi:greɪn]	Migräne
She gets migraines when the weather changes.	Sie bekommt Migräne, wenn sich das Wetter ändert.
miscarriage ['mɪskærɪdʒ]	Fehlgeburt
She really suffered after her last miscarriage.	Sie hat nach ihrer letzen Fehlgeburt sehr gelitten.
mucous ['mju:kəs]	Schleim
Her mucous membranes are infected.	Sie hat eine Schleimhautentzündung.
mumps [mʌmps]	Mumps
naturopathy ['nætʃʊr'ɔpəθɪ]	Naturheilkunde
nervous breakdown [nɜ:vəs 'breɪkdaʊn]	Nervenzusammenbruch
She had a nervous breakdown before her exams.	Sie erlitt vor ihren Prüfungen einen Nervenzusammenbruch.
neurosis [njʊə'rəʊsɪs]	Neurose
nosebleed ['nəʊsbli:d]	Nasenbluten
As a child, he often had nosebleeds.	Als Kind bekam er öfters Nasenbluten.
to observe [əb'zɜ:v]	beobachten
They are going to keep the patient overnight for observation.	Sie werden den Patienten zur Beobachtung über Nacht da behalten.

operation [ɔpəˈreɪʃən]	Operation; Eingriff
operating theatre [ˈɔpəreɪtɪŋ ˈθɪətə]	Operationssaal
The surgeon is already in the operating theatre.	Der Chirurg ist schon im Operationssaal.
outpatient [ˈaʊtpeɪʃənt]	ambulanter Patient
He will be treated as an outpatient.	Er wird als ambulanter Patient behandelt.
to palpate [pælˈpeɪt]	abtasten
The doctor palpated her ribs.	Der Arzt tastete ihre Rippen ab.
paralyzed [ˈpærəlaɪzd]	gelähmt
He is paralyzed in both legs.	Er ist in beiden Beinen gelähmt.
pathology [pəˈθɔlədʒi]	Pathologie
The corpse was taken to pathology.	Die Leiche wurde in die Pathologie gebracht.
patient [ˈpeɪʃənt]	Patient(in); geduldig
That patient is very patient and polite.	Jener Patient ist sehr geduldig und höflich.

False Friends

Watch out!

Pest in German is not the same as *pest* in English. *A pest* in English is *an annoying person*, while *die Pest* is translated as *plague*.

Ex: He is such a pest.

Er ist eine totale Nervensäge.

plague [pleɪg]	Pest
The plague killed many people in London.	Die Pest kostete in London viele Menschenleben.

Plague idioms

In English, you can't say *I hate something like the plague*. (German: etwas wie die Pest hassen). However, you can *avoid something like the plague* (etwas tunlichst vermeiden).

poisoning ['pɔɪsənɪŋ]	Vergiftung
She got food poisoning from the fish.	Sie bekam eine Lebensmittelvergiftung vom Fisch.
to pop [pɔp]	knallen; zerplatzen
premature baby ['premətjʊə 'beɪbɪ]	Frühgeburt
to prescribe [prɪ'skraɪb]	verschreiben
He prescribed her an antibiotic for her bronchitis.	Er verschrieb ihr ein Antibiotikum gegen ihre Bronchitis.
prescription [prɪ'skrɪpʃən]	Rezept
You need a prescription for that medicine.	Du brauchst für diese Medizin ein Rezept.
psychiatry [saɪ'kaɪətrɪ]	Psychiatrie
psychology [saɪ'kɔlədʒɪ]	Psychologie
pus [pʌs]	Eiter
The wound was full of pus.	Die Wunde war voller Eiter.

rash [ræʃ]	Ausschlag
She gets a rash when she is under stress.	Sie bekommt Ausschlag, wenn sie gestresst ist.
resuscitation [rɪ'sʌsɪteɪʃən]	Wiederbelebung
After pulling the child from the pool, they were able to resuscitate him.	Nachdem sie das Kind aus dem Pool gezogen haben, konnten sie es wiederbeleben.
rheumatism ['ruːmətɪzəm]	Rheuma
Her rheumatism has got worse in the past year.	Ihr Rheuma ist im Laufe dieses Jahres schlechter geworden.
schizophrenia [skɪtzəʊ'friːnɪə]	Schizophrenie
sedative ['sedətɪv]	Beruhigungsmittel
They gave her a sedative to help her sleep.	Sie haben ihr ein Beruhigungsmittel gegeben, so dass sie schlafen konnte.
short-sighted [ʃɔːt 'saɪtɪd]	kurzsichtig
specialist ['speʃəlɪst]	Spezialist(in); Facharzt; Fachärztin
I would see a specialist about your complaint.	Ich würde wegen deines Leidens einen Facharzt aufsuchen.
spontaneous [spɔn'teɪnɪəs]	spontan
to sprain [spreɪn]	verstauchen
He sprained his ankle playing football.	Er verstauchte sich den Knöchel beim Fußball.

stomach-ache ['stʌmək eɪk] Magenschmerzen
I had a stomach-ache after eating all that strawberry ice-cream. Ich hatte Magenschmerzen nach dem ganzen Erdbeereis.
stroke [strəʊk] Schlaganfall
He was never the same after his stroke. Er war nach seinem Schlaganfall nie wieder derselbe.

to subside [səb'saɪd] abklingen
The pain slowly subsided. Der Schmerz ist langsam abgeklungen.

superficial [suːpə'fɪʃəl] oberflächlich
The wound is only superficial. Die Wunde ist nur oberflächlich.
tablet ['tæblɪt] Tablette
tetanus ['tetənəs] Wundstarrkrampf; Tetanus
Have you been vaccinated against tetanus? Wurden Sie gegen Tetanus geimpft?
therapy ['θerəpɪ] Therapie
tonsillitis ['tɔnsɪ'laɪtɪs] Mandelentzündung
My sore throat turned into tonsillitis. Meine Halsschmerzen haben sich zu einer Mandelentzündung entwickelt.

tranquillizer ['træŋkwɪlaɪzə] Beruhigungsmittel
transfusion [træns'fjuːʃən] Transfusion
He lost so much blood that he needed a transfusion. Er hat so viel Blut verloren, dass er eine Transfusion brauchte.

transplant [træns'plɑːnt] — Transplantation
The liver is so badly damaged that he will need a transplant. — Die Leber ist so schwer geschädigt, dass er eine Transplantation brauchen wird.

to treat [triːt] — behandeln
They treated it with an anti-inflammatory drug. — Sie haben es mit einem entzündungshemmenden Mittel behandelt.

treatment ['triːtmənt] — Behandlung
The treatment seems to be working. — Die Behandlung scheint effektiv zu sein.

tumour ['tjuːmə] — Tumor

unconscious [ʌn'kɔnʃəs] — bewusstlos
She was unconscious when they brought her into the hospital. — Sie war bewusstlos, als sie sie ins Krankenhaus brachten.

to vaccinate [væksɪ'neɪt] — impfen
The whole city has been vaccinated against smallpox. — Die ganze Stadt wurde gegen Pocken geimpft.

venereal disease [vɪ'nɪərɪəl dɪ'ziːz] — Geschlechtskrankheit
You can get a venereal disease from unprotected sex! — Du kannst von ungeschütztem Sex eine Geschlechtskrankheit bekommen!

virus ['vaɪrəs] — Virus
The virus is spread through unclean water. — Der Virus wird durch unsauberes Wasser übertragen.

to vomit [vɔmɪt] — erbrechen
He drank so much that he had to vomit. — Er hat so viel getrunken, dass er erbrechen musste.
to wail [weɪl] — jammern
ward [wɔːd] — Station (Krankenhaus)
withdrawal [wɪð'drɔːəl] — Entzug
wound [wuːnd] — Wunde
The wound stopped bleeding after a few minutes. — Die Wunde hat nach ein paar Minuten aufgehört zu bluten.
The wound will need stitches. — Die Wunde muss genäht werden.
X-ray [eks reɪ] — Röntgenbild

Musik und Theater

1. Musik allgemein

bar [bɑː] — Takt
Let's start three bars from the top. — Fangen wir drei Takte nach dem Anfang an.
bass clef [beɪs klef] — Bass-Schlüssel
He can't read the bass clef! — Er kann keinen Bass-Schlüssel lesen!
chord [kɔːd] — Akkord
You struck the wrong chord. — Du hast den falschen Akkord angeschlagen.

to compose [kəm'pəʊz]	komponieren
He has composed several film scores.	Er hat schon mehrfach Filmmusik komponiert.
composer [kəm'pəʊzə]	Komponist(in)
crotchet [krɔtʃɪt]	Viertelnote
to dot [dɔt]	punktieren
Dotted notes should be held longer.	Punktierte Noten sollten länger gehalten werden.
flat [flæt]	B-Vorzeichen
That note has a flat in front of it.	Die Note hat ein B-Vorzeichen.
fugue [fjuːg]	Fuge
Bach was famous for his fugues.	Bach war für seine Fugen bekannt.
harmony ['hɑːmənɪ]	Harmonie; Harmonielehre
key [kiː]	Tonart; Taste
What key is the sonata in?	In welcher Tonart ist die Sonate geschrieben?
key signature [kiː'sɪgnətʃə]	Vorzeichen
major ['meɪdʒə]	Dur
melody ['melədɪ]	Melodie
The melody of those two arias is almost the same.	Die Melodie dieser zwei Arien ist fast gleich.
minim ['mɪnɪm]	halbe Note
minor ['maɪnə]	Moll
The overture is in B-flat minor.	Die Ouvertüre ist in b-Moll.
note [nəʊt]	Note; Ton

False Friends

Watch out! A German musical *Note* has the same meaning as an English musical *note*. However, if you are talking about school, you do not get *notes* on your tests, but *grades* or *marks*.

octave ['ɔktɪv]	Oktave
His hand can reach an entire octave on the piano.	Seine Hand kann am Klavier eine ganze Oktave umspannen.
overture ['əʊvətjʊə]	Ouvertüre
People continued to talk during the overture.	Das Publikum redete während der Ouvertüre weiter.
quaver ['kweɪvə]	Achtelnote
rest [rest]	Pause
There is a rest at the end of the bar.	Es gibt eine Pause am Ende des Taktes.
rhythm ['rɪðəm]	Rhythmus
The rhythm is rather complicated.	Der Rhythmus ist ziemlich kompliziert.
scale [skeɪl]	Tonleiter
score [skɔː]	Partitur; Noten
He studied the score for three weeks.	Drei Wochen lang studierte er die Partitur ein.
semibreve ['semɪ briːv]	ganze Note
sharp [ʃɑːp]	Kreuz
Didn't you see the sharp in front of the E?	Hast du das Kreuz vor dem E nicht gesehen?

sonata [sə'nɑːtə]	Sonate
Beethoven's "Moonlight Sonata" is very well-loved.	Beethovens „Mondschein Sonate" ist sehr beliebt.
symphony ['sɪmfənɪ]	Sinfonie
Mozart wrote symphonies for Prague, Paris and Linz.	Mozart schrieb Sinfonien für Prag, Paris und Linz.
time [taɪm]	Takt
tone [təʊn]	Ton; Ganzton
tune [tjuːn]	Melodie
I know this tune from somewhere.	Ich kenne diese Melodie irgendwoher.

2. Instrumente und Gesang

accordion [ə'kɔːdɪən]	Akkordeon
alto ['æltəʊ]	Alt; Altstimme
to audition [ɔː'dɪʃən]	vorsingen; vorstellen
audition [ɔː'dɪʃən]	Vorsingen; Vorstellung
She has an audition at the Metropolitan Opera.	Sie muss an der Metropolitan Opera vorsingen.
baritone ['bærɪtəʊn]	Bariton
Wotan is a popular baritone role.	Wotan ist eine beliebte Bariton-Partie.
bass [beɪs]	Bass
brass band [brɑːs bænd]	Blaskapelle
Several brass bands play at the Octoberfest.	Mehrere Blaskapellen spielen auf dem Oktoberfest.

canon ['kænən]	Kanon
A canon often has three parts.	Ein Kanon hat häufig drei Partien.
cello ['tʃeləʊ]	Cello
He has a cello made by …	Er hat ein Cello, das von … gefertigt wurde.
chamber concert ['tʃeɪmbə 'kɔnsət]	Kammerkonzert
There are often chamber concerts at the castle.	Das Schloss bietet öfters Kammerkonzerte an.
chamber music ['tʃeɪmbə 'mjuːzɪk]	Kammermusik
They often play chamber music at home.	Sie machen zu Hause oft Kammermusik.
chapel ['tʃæpəl]	Kapelle
The chapel echoed with the noise.	Das Geräusch hallte durch die Kapelle.
choir [kwaɪə]	Chor
The church choir is quite good.	Der Kirchenchor ist sehr gut.
chorale [kə'rɑːl]	Choral
"A Mighty Fortress is our God" is a well-known Bach chorale.	„Eine feste Burg ist unser Gott" ist ein bekannter Choral von Bach.
clarinet [klærɪ'net]	Klarinette
He played the clarinet in a jazz band.	Er spielte in einer Jazzband Klarinette.
concert ['kɔnsət]	Konzert

The concert was a great success.	Das Konzert war ein Riesenerfolg.
to conduct [kən'dʌkt]	dirigieren
He has conducted the Vienna Philharmonic for many years.	Er dirigiert die Wiener Philharmoniker seit vielen Jahren.
conductor [kən'dʌktə]	Dirigent(in)
The conductor threw his baton in a rage.	In seinem Zorn warf der Dirigent seinen Stab von sich.
duet ['djuːet]	Duett
That is the loveliest duet in the entire opera.	Dies ist das schönste Duett in der ganzen Oper.
flute [fluːt]	Querflöte
grand piano [grænd pɪ'ænəʊ]	Flügel
A grand piano is too large for our living room.	Ein Flügel ist zu groß für unser Wohnzimmer.
guitar [gɪ'tɑː]	Gitarre
harp [hɑːp]	Harfe
The harp is my favourite instrument.	Die Harfe ist mein Lieblingsinstrument.
harpsichord ['hɑːpsɪkɔːd]	Cembalo
instrument ['ɪnstrʊmənt]	Instrument
kettle-drum ['ketl drʌm]	Pauke
The kettle-drum was very loud.	Die Pauke war sehr laut.
lullaby ['lʌləbaɪ]	Wiegenlied

She sings a lullaby to her baby every night.	Sie singt ihrem Baby jeden Abend ein Wiegenlied.
orchestra ['ɔːkɪstrə]	Orchester
The orchestra was not playing together.	Das Orchester hat nicht zusammengespielt.
organ ['ɔːgən]	Orgel
The church has got a new organ.	Die Kirche hat eine neue Orgel.
percussion [pə'kʌʃən]	Schlagzeug
He studies percussion at the conservatory.	Er studiert am Konservatorium Schlagzeug.
piano [pɪ'ænəʊ]	Klavier
recorder [rɪ'kɔːdə]	Blockflöte
Many children in Germany learn the recorder.	Viele Kinder in Deutschland lernen Blockflöte.
saxophone ['sæksəfəʊn]	Saxofon
The saxophone is often used in jazz music.	Das Saxofon wird oft in der Jazzmusik benutzt.
solo ['səʊləʊ]	Solo
soloist ['səʊləʊɪst]	Solist(in)
soprano [sə'prɑːnəʊ]	Sopran
The soprano was very good last night.	Der Sopran gestern Abend war sehr gut.
string [strɪŋ]	Saite
He broke a string during the concert.	Während des Konzerts ist eine seiner Saiten gerissen.
strings [strɪŋz]	Streicher
tenor ['tenə]	Tenor

Siegfried is a famous tenor role.	Siegfried ist eine bekannte Tenor-Partie.
trombone [trɔm'bəʊn]	Posaune
trumpet ['trʌmpɪt]	Trompete
to tune [tjuːn]	stimmen
We all tuned our instruments and waited for the concert to begin.	Wir haben alle unsere Instrumente gestimmt und warteten auf den Beginn des Konzerts.
upright piano ['ʌpraɪt pɪ'ænəʊ]	Klavier
viola [vɪ'əʊlə]	Bratsche
violin [vaɪə'lɪn]	Geige; Violine
vocal ['vəʊkəl]	gesanglich; Vokal-
She doesn't like vocal music.	Ihr gefällt Vokalmusik nicht.
wind instrument [wɪnd 'ɪnstrʊmənt]	Blasinstrument
The oboe, clarinet and flute are wind instruments.	Oboe, Klarinette und Querflöte sind Blasinstrumente.

3. Theater

act [ækt]	Akt; Aufzug
acting ['æktɪŋ]	Schauspielerei
Her acting was very bad.	Ihre Schauspielerei war sehr schlecht.
actor ['æktə]	Schauspieler

That actor hasn't made a good film in years.	Dieser Schauspieler hat seit Jahren keinen guten Film mehr gemacht.
actress ['æktrɪs]	Schauspielerin
amphitheatre ['æmfɪθɪətə]	Amphitheater
The show in the amphitheatre was cancelled because of the rain.	Die Show im Amphitheater wurde wegen Regen abgesagt.
appearance [ə'pɪərəns]	Auftritt
applause [ə'plɔːz]	Applaus
The applause was deafening.	Der Applaus war ohrenbetäubend.
audience ['ɔːdɪəns]	Zuschauer(in); Zuhörer(in); Publikum
The audience laughed.	Die Zuschauer lachten.
balcony ['bælkənɪ]	Galerie
The student seats are in the balcony.	Die Studentenplätze sind auf der Galerie.
box [bɔks]	Loge
Box seats are very expensive.	Logenplätze sind sehr teuer.
bow [bəʊ]	Bogen
to bow [baʊ]	sich verbeugen; sich verneigen
He bowed to the audience.	Er verneigte sich vor dem Publikum.
to bow one's head	den Kopf senken
cabaret ['kæbəreɪ]	Kabarett

comedy ['kɔmədɪ]	Komödie
The comedy wasn't very funny.	Die Komödie war nicht sehr witzig.
costume ['kɔstjuːm]	Kostüm
The costumes were very authentic.	Die Kostüme waren sehr authentisch.
curtain ['kɜːtn]	Vorhang
The curtain went up too soon.	Der Vorhang öffnete sich zu früh.
debut ['deɪbjuː]	Debüt
Tonight is her debut at this theatre.	Heute Abend ist ihr Debüt an diesem Theater.
director [dɪ'rektə]	Regisseur(in)
The director is well-respected in France.	Der Regisseur ist in Frankreich hoch angesehen.
drama ['drɑːmə]	Drama
dress-rehearsal [dres rɪ'hɜːsəl]	Generalprobe
The dress-rehearsal didn't go very well.	Die Generalprobe ist nicht sehr gut gelaufen.
encore ['ɔŋkɔː]	Zugabe
He gave three encores.	Er hat drei Zugaben gegeben.
extra ['ekstrə]	Statist(in)
He is an extra at the opera house.	Er ist Statist am Opernhaus.
hero ['hɪərəʊ]	Held
heroine ['herəʊɪn]	Heldin

The heroine dies at the end of the play.	Die Heldin stirbt am Ende des Stücks.
interval ['ɪntəvəl]	Pause
make-up [meɪk ʌp]	Schminke; Maske
The make-up was very convincing.	Die Maske war sehr überzeugend.
marionette [mærɪə'net]	Marionette
The marionette theater is popular with children.	Das Marionettentheater ist bei Kindern sehr beliebt.
masque [mɑːsk]	Maskenspiel
monologue ['mɔnəlɔg]	Monolog
music hall ['mjuːzɪk hɔːl]	Varieté
one-act play [wʌn ækt pleɪ]	Einakter
"Salome" is an one-act play by Oscar Wilde.	„Salome" ist ein Einakter von Oscar Wilde.
opera ['ɔprə]	Oper
She loves going to the opera.	Sie geht unheimlich gern in die Oper.
opera glasses ['ɔprə 'glɑːsɪz]	Opernglas
pantomime ['pæntəmaɪm]	Pantomime
performance [pə'fɔːməns]	Aufführung
Last night's performance was better than tonight's.	Die Aufführung gestern Abend war besser als die von heute Abend.
production [prə'dʌkʃən]	Inszenierung
He doesn't like modern productions.	Er mag keine modernen Inszenierungen.

to prompt [prɔmpt]	soufflieren
After her singing career was over, she worked as a prompter.	Nachdem ihre Karriere als Sängerin vorbei war, arbeitete sie als Souffleuse.
rehearsal [rɪ'hɜːsəl]	Probe
The rehearsal went on late into the night.	Die Probe ging bis spät in die Nacht.
to rehearse [rɪ'hɜːs]	proben
role [rəʊl]	Rolle
Lady Macbeth is her dream role.	Lady Macbeth ist ihre Traumrolle.
season ['siːzən]	Spielzeit
The season goes from September till June.	Die Spielzeit geht von September bis Juni.
sound effects [saʊnd ɪ'fekts]	Geräusche
stage [steɪdʒ]	Bühne
The stage was completely dark.	Die Bühne war komplett dunkel.
stalls [stɔːlz]	Parkett
standing room ['stændɪŋ ruːm]	Stehplätze
theatre ['θɪətər]	Theater
The theatre was burned to the ground.	Das Theater ist abgebrannt.
theatre company	Theaterensemble
theatre critic	Theaterkritiker(in)
tragedy ['trædʒədɪ]	Tragödie

Politik und Gesellschaft

1. Gesellschaft

assassination [əsæsɪ'neɪʃən]	Attentat
He survived the assassination attempt.	Er überlebte das Attentat.
class [klɑːs]	Schicht
She comes from the upper class.	Sie kommt aus der Oberschicht.
demonstration [demən'streɪʃən]	Demonstration
to hold a demonstration	eine Demonstration durchführen
emigration [emɪ'greɪʃən]	Aus-/Abwanderung
The country is suffering from the emigration of its brightest students.	Das Land leidet unter der Abwanderung seiner besten Studenten.
extremism [ɪk'striːmɪzəm]	Extremismus
Many countries are afraid of extremists.	Viele Länder haben Angst vor Extremisten.
immigration [ɪmɪ'greɪʃən]	Einwanderung
The United States is a country of immigrants.	Die USA ist ein Land von Einwanderern.
Labour (UK) ['leɪbə]	Arbeiterpartei
Labour is successful in Britain.	Die Arbeiterpartei ist in Großbritannien erfolgreich.

left-wing [left wɪŋ]	links
He was very left-wing during his student days.	Er war während seiner Studienzeit sehr links-orientiert.
majority [mə'dʒɔrɪtɪ]	Mehrheit
They lost the majority in Parliament.	Sie haben die Mehrheit im Parlament verloren.
militant ['mɪlɪtənt]	kämpferisch; militant
minority [maɪ'nɔrɪtɪ]	Minderheit
The Chinese are a minority in Malaysia.	Die Chinesen sind in Malaysia in der Minderheit.
naturalization [nætʃrəlaɪ'zeɪʃən]	Einbürgerung
The government has passed new naturalization laws.	Die Regierung hat neue Einbürgerungsgesetze verabschiedet.
population [pɔpjʊ'leɪʃən]	Bevölkerung
racism ['reɪsɪzəm]	Rassismus
Many countries have problems with racism.	Viele Länder haben Probleme mit Rassismus.
right-wing [raɪt wɪŋ]	rechts
settlement ['setlmənt]	Beilegung (eines Streits)
The company and the union reached a settlement.	Die Firma und die Gewerkschaft haben sich für eine Beilegung des Streits entschlossen.
society [sə'saɪətɪ]	Gesellschaft
union ['juːnjən]	Gewerkschaft

2. Staat und Verwaltung

to abdicate ['æbdɪkeɪt]	abdanken
The king abdicated in order to marry.	Der König dankte ab, um zu heiraten.
act [ækt]	Gesetz
administration [ædmɪnɪ'streɪʃən]	Verwaltung
The administration takes care of that.	Die Verwaltung kümmert sich darum.
ballot paper ['bælət peɪpɔ]	Wahlzettel
The ballot paper is very confusing.	Der Wahlzettel ist sehr verwirrend.
basic law ['beɪsɪk lɔː]	Grundgesetz
bill [bil]	Gesetzentwurf; (Gesetzes)Vorlage
The bill proposes a tax increase.	Der Gesetzentwurf schlägt eine Steuererhöhung vor.
budget ['bʌdʒɪt]	(Staats)Haushalt
There is not enough room in the budget for more spending.	Der Haushalt hat für mehr Ausgaben nicht genug Geld.
bureaucracy [bjuː'rɔkrəsɪ]	Bürokratie
Dealing with bureaucracy can be very frustrating.	Es kann frustrierend sein, wenn man mit der Bürokratie in Berührung kommt.

cabinet ['kæbɪnət]	Kabinett
His cabinet members are carefully selected.	Die Mitglieder seines Kabinetts sind sorgfältig ausgewählt.
cabinet meeting ['kæbɪnət 'miːtɪŋ]	Kabinettssitzung
campaign [kæm'peɪn]	Wahlkampf
candidate ['kændɪdət]	Kandidat(in)
He was not the party's ideal candidate.	Er war nicht der Wunschkandidat der Partei.
chancellor ['tʃɑːnsələ]	Kanzler
Helmut Kohl was the chancellor of Germany for many years.	Helmut Kohl war in Deutschland für viele Jahre Kanzler.
Chancellor of the Exchequer (UK) ['tʃɑːnsələ əv ðiː ɪks'tʃekə]	Finanzminister
civic ['sɪvɪk]	staatsbürgerlich
coalition [kəʊə'lɪʃən]	Koalition; Vereinigung
The coalition is falling apart.	Die Koalition bricht auseinander.
committee [kə'mɪtɪ]	Ausschuss
The investigation committee will present its results tomorrow.	Der Untersuchungsausschuss wird seine Ergebnisse morgen darlegen.
community [kə'mjuːnɪtɪ]	Gemeinde
The community is against the initiative.	Die Gemeinde ist gegen die Initiative.

conservative [kən'sɜːvətɪv]	Konservative(r); konservativ
He is very conservative in his religious beliefs.	Er ist sehr konservativ in seinem Glauben.
constitution [kɔnstɪ'tjuːʃən]	Verfassung; Grundgesetz
Those rights are guaranteed under the constitution.	Diese Rechte sind im Grundgesetz verankert.
currency reform ['kʌrənsɪ rɪ'fɔːm]	Währungsreform
debate [dɪ'beɪt]	Debatte
The debate will be aired at 8 p.m.	Die Debatte wird um 20 Uhr ausgestrahlt.
dissident ['dɪsɪdənt]	Dissident(in); Abtrünnige(r)
The dissident spent many years in prison.	Der Dissident verbrachte viele Jahre im Gefängnis.
domestic policy [də'mestɪk 'pɔlɪsɪ]	Innenpolitik
draft [drɑːft]	Entwurf
economic policy [iːkə'nɔmɪk 'pɔlɪsɪ]	Wirtschaftspolitik
His economic policy is disappointing.	Seine Wirtschaftspolitik ist enttäuschend.
to elect [ɪ'lekt]	wählen; stimmen für
The country elected a new Prime Minister.	Das Land wählte einen neuen Premierminister.
election [ɪ'lekʃən]	Wahl
We are waiting for the election results.	Wir warten auf die Wahlergebnisse.

election campaign [ɪ'lekʃən kæm'peɪn]	Wahlkampf
He made many promises during his election campaign.	Er hat während seines Wahlkampfs viele Versprechen gegeben.
election result [ɪ'lekʃən rɪ'sʌlt]	Wahlergebnis
Federal Chancellor ['fedərəl 'tʃɑːnsələ]	Bundeskanzler
federation [fedə'reɪʃən]	Bund; Föderation
The federation is made up of the four states.	Der Bund besteht aus den vier Bundesstaaten.
fiscal policy ['fɪskəl 'pɔlɪsɪ]	Finanzpolitik
The party's fiscal policy is very conservative.	Die Finanzpolitik der Partei ist sehr konservativ.
Home Office (UK) [həʊm 'ɔfɪs]	Innenministerium
The Home Office has issued a warning.	Das Innenministerium hat eine Warnung ausgesprochen.
House of Representatives [haʊs əv reprɪ'zentətɪvz]	Repräsentantenhaus
The House of Representatives vetoed the bill.	Das Repräsentantenhaus (in USA) lehnte den Gesetzentwurf ab.
Houses of Parliament [haʊziz əv 'pɑːləmənt]	Abgeordnetenhaus (in Großbritannien)
judge [dʒʌdʒ]	Richter(in)

The judge barred all reporters from the trial.	Der Richter schloss alle Journalisten vom Prozess aus.
jurisdiction [dʒʊərɪs'dɪkʃən]	Rechtsprechung
law [lɔː]	Gesetz
We have to obey the laws.	Wir müssen den Gesetzen Folge leisten.
law court	Gerichtshof; Gericht
law-abiding	gesetzestreu
legislation [ledʒɪs'leɪʃən]	Gesetzgebung
liberal ['lɪbərəl]	Liberale(r); liberal
He is very liberal regarding moral issues.	Er ist sehr liberal, was ethische Fragen betrifft.
local council ['ləʊkəl 'kaʊnsəl]	Gemeinderat
mandate ['mændeɪt]	Mandat
Member of Parliament ['membə əv 'pɑːləmənt]	Abgeordnete(r)
minister ['mɪnɪstə]	Minister(in)
Minister of Finance ['mɪnɪstə əv faɪ'næns]	Finanzminister(in)
The Minister of Finance will present the new fiscal policy.	Der Finanzminister wird die neue Finanzpolitik darlegen.
ministry ['mɪnɪstrɪ]	Ministerium
during his ministry	während seiner Amtszeit
Ministry of the Interior (US) ['mɪnɪstrɪ əv ðə ɪn'tɪərɪə]	Innenministerium

Some parts of the American government system
Ministry of the Interior: Innenministerium
Supreme Court: Oberster Gerichtshof
The Pentagon: Verteidigungsministerium
The Federal Bureau of Investigation (FBI): Bundespolizei
The Electoral College: Wahlmänner

minutes ['mɪnɪts]	Sitzungsprotokoll
municipal [mjuː'nɪsɪpəl]	Stadt-; Gemeinde-
municipal council [mjuː'nɪsɪpəl kaʊnsl]	Stadtrat
The municipal council will discuss the plans for the new stadium.	Der Stadtrat wird die Pläne für ein neues Stadion besprechen.
municipal election [mjuː'nɪsɪpəl ɪ'lekʃən]	Kommunalwahl
opponent [ə'pəʊnənt]	Gegenkandidat(in)
He has more experience than his opponent.	Er hat mehr Erfahrung als sein Gegner.
opposition [ɔpə'zɪʃən]	Opposition
parliament ['pɑːləmənt]	Parlament
party ['pɑːtɪ]	Partei
He is not a member of either party.	Er ist Mitglied bei keiner der beiden Parteien.
petition [pə'tɪʃən]	Eingabe; Antrag
policy ['pɔlɪsɪ]	Politik
There has been a change in the foreign policy.	Es gab eine Veränderung in der Außenpolitik.

Prime Minister ['praɪm 'mɪnɪstə]	Premierminister(in)
referendum [refə'rendəm]	Volksabstimmung
to resign [rɪ'zaɪn]	zurücktreten; abdanken
He resigned after the news of his affair broke.	Er ist zurückgetreten, nachdem die Öffentlichkeit von seiner Affäre erfuhr.
senate ['senɪt]	Senat
sitting ['sɪtɪŋ]	Sitzung
social democracy ['səʊʃl dɪ'mɔkrəsɪ]	Sozialdemokratie
to vote [vəʊt]	wählen
It is important that every citizen votes.	Es ist wichtig, dass jeder Bürger wählt.
welfare state ['welfɛə steɪt]	Sozialstaat

3. Weltpolitik, Krieg und Frieden

alliance [ə'laɪəns]	Bündnis; Vereinigung
The countries formed an alliance against their mutual enemy.	Die Länder schlossen sich zu einem Bündnis gegen den gemeinsamen Feind zusammen.
ambassador [æm'bæsədə]	Botschafter(in)
The ambassador received the delegation.	Der Botschafter empfing die Delegation.
to annex [ə'neks]	annektieren
arbitration [ɑːbɪ'treɪʃən]	Schiedsgerichtswesen

arms race [ɑːms reɪs]	Wettrüsten
The arms race between the United States and the Soviet Union ended in the 90's.	Das Wettrüsten zwischen den USA und der Sowjetunion endete in den 90er Jahren.
bilateral [baɪ'lætərəl]	bilateral
border ['bɔːdə]	Grenze
boycott ['bɔɪkɔt]	Boykott
consul ['kɔnsl]	Konsul(in)
consulate ['kɔnsjʊlət]	Konsulat
You can get a new passport at the consulate.	Du kannst beim Konsulat einen neuen Pass bekommen.
delegate ['delɪgeɪt]	Delegierte(r)
to demilitarize [dɪ'mɪlɪtəraɪz]	entmilitarisieren
They will try to demilitarize the country without using much force.	Sie werden versuchen, das Land zu entmilitarisieren, ohne viel Gewalt anzuwenden.
Department of Defence (US) [dɪ'pɑːtmənt əv dɪ'fens]	Verteidigungsministerium
détente [deɪ'tɑːnt]	Entspannungspolitik
diplomat ['dɪpləmæt]	Diplomat(in)
diplomatic immunity [dɪplə'mætɪk ɪm'juːnɪtɪ]	Immunität
The dictator was granted diplomatic immunity.	Dem Diktator wurde Immunität gewährt.

embargo [ɪm'bɑːgəʊ]	Embargo; Sperre
embassy ['embəsɪ]	Botschaft
The police stormed the embassy.	Die Polizei stürmte die Botschaft.
European Free Trade Association (EFTA) [jʊərə'pɪən friː treɪd əsəʊsɪ'eɪʃən]	Europäische Freihandelsgemeinschaft
European Parliament [jʊərə'pɪən pɑːləmənt]	Europaparlament
European Union (EU) [jʊərə'pɪən juːniːən]	Europäische Union
Is Norway a member of the EU?	Ist Norwegen ein Mitglied der EU?
foreign affairs ['fɔrən ə'fɛərs]	Außenpolitik
Foreign Minister ['fɔrən 'mɪnɪstə]	Außenminister(in)
The new Foreign Minister was once an ambassador.	Der neue Außenminister war einst Botschafter.
intelligence service [ɪn'telɪdʒəns 'sɜːvɪs]	Geheimdienst
The intelligence service discovered the assassination plot yesterday.	Der Geheimdienst entdeckte gestern die Attentatspläne.
Ministry of Defence (UK) ['mɪnɪstrɪ əv dɪ'fens]	Verteidigungsministerium

Ministry for Foreign Affairs ['mɪnɪstrɪ fɔː 'fɔrən ə'fɛəz]	Außenministerium
negotiate [nɪ'gəʊʃɪeɪt]	verhandeln; aushandeln
They will try to negotiate for the hostages' release.	Sie werden versuchen, die Freilassung der Geiseln auszuhandeln.
neutral ['njuːtrəl]	neutral
Switzerland has traditionally been a neutral country.	Die Schweiz ist schon immer ein neutrales Land gewesen.
pact [pækt]	Pakt
The two countries concluded a pact.	Die zwei Länder schlossen einen Pakt.
peace conference [piːs 'kɔnfərəns]	Friedenskonferenz
peace treaty [piːs 'triːtɪ]	Friedensvertrag
They broke the peace treaty by invading the island.	Sie haben den Friedensvertrag verletzt, indem sie die Insel angriffen.
ratification [rætɪfɪ'keɪʃən]	Ratifizierung
The treaty must be ratified.	Der Vertrag muss ratifiziert werden.
refugee [refjʊ'dʒiː]	Flüchtling
reunification [riːjuːnɪfɪ'keɪʃən]	Wiedervereinigung
secession [sɪ'seʃən]	Abspaltung
During the Civil War, the Southern states seceded	Während des amerikanischen Bürgerkriegs

from the Union.	spalteten sich die Südstaaten vom Bund ab.
self-determination [self dɪtɜːmɪ'neɪʃən]	Selbstbestimmung
self-government [self 'gʌvənmənt]	Selbstverwaltung
summit ['sʌmɪt]	Gipfel
summit meeting ['sʌmɪt 'miːtɪŋ]	Gipfeltreffen
superpower [suːpə'paʊə]	Großmacht
China has become a superpower.	China ist zu einer Großmacht geworden.
trade agreement [treɪd ə'griːmənt]	Handelsabkommen
They have a special trade agreement with Japan.	Sie haben ein besonderes Handelsabkommen mit Japan.
treaty ['triːtɪ]	Vertrag
treaty port	Vertragshafen

Plurals

Usually, forming the plural in English is easy: just add *s* or *es*. However, if a word ends in a consonant + *y*, the *y* is substituted with an *ie* and then the *s* is added.
Ex: treaty: treaties; army: armies; fly: flies; money: monies; lady: ladies; hobby: hobbies.
If a word ends in a vowel + *y* the *s* is just added!
Ex: day: days; boy: boys; valley: valleys.

4. Herrschaftsformen und Macht

anarchy ['ænəkɪ]	Anarchie
autocracy [ɔː'tɔkrəsɪ]	Alleinherrschaft
coup [kuː]	Putsch
The general siezed power through a military coup.	Der General riss die Macht mittels eines Putsches an sich.
democracy [dɪ'mɔkrəsɪ]	Demokratie
to deport [dɪ'pɔːt]	abschieben; ausweisen
He was deported after being sentenced.	Er wurde nach seiner Verurteilung ausgewiesen.
dictator [dɪk'teɪtə]	Diktator
The dictator is trying to hold on to his power.	Der Diktator versucht, an seiner Macht festzuhalten.
dictatorship [dɪk'teɪtaʃɪp]	Diktatur
exile ['eksaɪl]	Exil; Verbannung
Napoleon was exiled to Elba.	Napoleon wurde auf Elba verbannt.
to govern ['gʌvən]	regieren
The king governs with compassion.	Der König regiert mit Gnade.
government ['gʌvənmənt]	Regierung
power ['paʊə]	Macht
riot ['raɪət]	Aufruhr
There was a riot after the law was passed.	Es gab einen Aufruhr, nachdem das Gesetz verabschiedet war.

Government synonyms

govern: rule
treaty: agreement
alliance: confederation
ratify: approve
arbitrate: mediate
delegate: assign

Reisen, Hotels und Gastronomie

1. Reisen und Hotels

accommodation [əkɔmə'deɪʃən]	Unterkunft
The sponsor will provide accomodation.	Der Sponsor wird die Unterkunft zur Verfügung stellen.
agenda [ə'dʒendə]	Tagesordnung; Programm
What is on the agenda for today?	Was steht heute auf der Tagesordnung?
airline ['ɛəlaɪn]	Fluggesellschaft
airport ['ɛəpɔːt]	Flughafen
The airport was closed due to bad weather.	Der Flughafen wurde wegen schlechten Wetters geschlossen.
arrival [ə'raɪvəl]	Ankunft
His arrival was delayed.	Seine Ankuft wurde verzögert.
bar [bɑː]	Bar
bedding ['bedɪŋ]	Bettwäsche

The bedding was dirty.	Die Bettwäsche war schmutzig.
booking ['bʊkɪŋ]	Buchung
bureau de change ['bjuːrəʊ də tʃeɪndʒ]	Wechselstube
charter flight ['tʃɑːtə flaɪt]	Charterflug
They took a charter flight to Tunesia.	Sie sind mit einem Charterflug nach Tunesien geflogen.
check in [tʃek ɪn]	Abfertigung; Check-In
coach [kəʊtʃ]	Reisebus
customs ['kʌstəmz]	Zoll
You will never get that through customs!	Du wirst das nie durch den Zoll bekommen!
delay [dɪ'leɪ]	Verspätung
I missed my connecting flight because my first plane was delayed.	Ich habe meinen Anschlussflug verpasst, weil mein erster Flug Verspätung hatte.
economy class [ɪ'kɔnəmɪ klɑːs]	Economyklasse
The economy class is full.	Die Economyklasse ist ausgebucht.
first class [fɜːst klɑːs]	erste Klasse
flight [flaɪt]	Flug
full board [fʊl bɔːd]	Vollpension
The price includes full board.	Vollpension ist im Preis inbegriffen.

guide [gaɪd]	Reiseführer
We hired a guide to show us around Munich.	Wir haben einen Reiseführer angeheuert, der uns München zeigt.
itinerary [aɪ'tɪnərərɪ]	Reiseplan
Our itinerary has no room for changes.	Unser Reiseplan lässt keinen Raum für Änderungen zu.
lift [lɪft]	Aufzug
lift attendant	Fahrstuhlführer
maid [meɪd]	Zimmermädchen
I think the maid took my ring.	Ich fürchte, das Zimmermädchen hat meinen Ring genommen.
map [mæp]	Stadtplan
Do you have a map of Paris?	Hast du einen Stadtplan von Paris?

False Friends

Watch out! *Map* and *Mappe* are not the same thing.
Mappe translated into English is *portfolio* or *folder*.
Ex: She brought her portfolio to the interview.
Sie brachte ihre Mappe zum Interview mit.

menu ['menjuː]	Speisekarte
There seems to be nothing without meat on the menu.	Es scheint auf der Speisekarte nichts Fleischloses zu geben.

passenger ['pæsɪndʒə]	Passagier; Fahrgast
passport ['pɑːspɔːt]	Reisepass
She had to get a new passport after hers was stolen.	Sie musste sich einen neuen Reisepass holen, nachdem ihrer geklaut wurde.
passport control	Passkontrolle
porter ['pɔːtə]	Gepäckträger
to reserve [rɪ'zɜːv]	reservieren
I would like to reserve two rooms.	Ich würde gerne zwei Zimmer reservieren.
room service [ruːm 'sɜːvɪs]	Zimmerservice
Call room service if you are hungry!	Ruf den Zimmerservice an, wenn du Hunger hast!
sight-seeing tour [saɪt 'siːɪŋ tʊə]	Stadtrundfahrt
station ['steɪʃən]	Bahnhof
She will be at the station at three.	Sie wird um drei am Bahnhof sein.
stopover ['stɔpəʊvə]	Zwischenlandung
We have a stopover in Baltimore.	Wir haben eine Zwischenlandung in Baltimore.
supplement ['sʌplɪmənt]	Zuschlag
tour guide [tʊə gaɪd]	Reiseleiter(in)
tourist ['tʊərɪst]	Tourist(in)
tourist party ['tʊərɪst 'pɑːtɪ]	Reisegesellschaft
travel ['trævl]	Reisen
The job requires a lot of travelling.	Der Job erfordert viel Reisen.

travel agency ['trævl 'eɪdʒənsɪ]	Reisebüro
The travel agency got me the best price.	Das Reisebüro hat mir den besten Preis herausgesucht.
traveller's cheque ['trævləz tʃek]	Reisescheck
Sign your traveller's cheques!	Unterschreib deine Reiseschecks!

British and American spelling

British	*American*
cheque	check
colour	color (most words with *ou* are the same)
centre	center (also theater, kilometer etc.)

travelling bag ['trævəlɪŋ bæg]	Reisetasche
travelling expenses ['trævəlɪŋ ɪk'spensəz]	Reisekosten
trip [trɪp]	Reise
view point ['vjuːpɔɪnt]	Aussichtspunkt
From the view point you can see the mountains.	Vom Aussichtspunkt aus kannst du die Berge sehen.
youth-hostel [juːθ 'hɔstəl]	Jugendherberge
The youth-hostel also has a disco.	Die Jugendherberge hat auch eine Disko.

2. Gastronomie

alcohol ['ælkəhɔl]	Alkohol
He doesn't drink alcohol.	Er trinkt keinen Alkohol.
appetizer [æpɪtaɪzə]	Vorspeise

Some (fattening) American appetizers
mozarella sticks: panierte Käsestangen mit Dip
onion rings: Zwiebelringe
potato skins: gewürzte, frittierte Kartoffelstücke
chicken wings: Hühnerflügel mit verschiedenen Soßen

apricot ['eɪprɪkɔt]	Aprikose
The apricot is not ripe.	Die Aprikose ist nicht reif.
artificial sweetener ['ɑːtɪfɪʃəl 'swiːtnə]	Süßstoff
avocado [ævə'kɑːdəʊ]	Avocado
Guacamole is made from avocado.	Guacamole wird aus Avocado gemacht.
baby-food ['beɪbɪ fuːd]	Säuglingsnahrung
bacon ['beɪkən]	Frühstücksspeck
I love the smell of bacon and egg.	Ich liebe den Geruch von Ei und Frühstücksspeck.
to bake [beɪk]	backen
baked apples	Bratäpfel
baking powder [beɪkɪŋ 'paʊdə]	Backpulver
baking tin ['beɪkɪŋ tɪn]	Backform

You should grease the baking tin!	Du solltest die Backform einfetten!
bar [bɑː]	Riegel
Would you like a chocolate bar?	Möchtest du einen Schokoriegel?
beaten egg white ['biːtən eg waɪt]	Eischnee
Mix the beaten egg white and the cream together!	Mischen Sie den Eischnee mit der Sahne!
beef [biːf]	Rindfleisch
She is afraid to eat beef after the whole BSE crisis.	Nach der BSE Krise hat sie Angst, Rindfleich zu essen.
beverage ['bevərɪdʒ]	Getränk
biscuit ['bɪskɪt]	Plätzchen; Keks

British and American food

In the US, *biscuits* are called *cookies*. *Potato chips* are called *crisps* in Britain and *British chips* are *fries* in the US.

bitter ['bɪtə]	bitter
black tea [blæk tiː]	schwarzer Tee
Earl Grey is a well-known sort of black tea.	Earl Grey ist ein bekannter Schwarztee.
boiling ['bɔɪlɪŋ]	siedend
brandy ['brændɪ]	Weinbrand
They brought a nice brandy from France.	Sie haben einen edlen Weinbrand aus Frankreich mitgebracht.

breadcrumbs [bredkrʌms]	Paniermehl; Semmelbrösel
The chicken was dipped in breadcrumbs.	Das Huhn wurde in Paniermehl gewendet.
caffeine ['kæfiːn]	Koffein
can/tin [kæn/tɪn]	Dose; Büchse
The can has a dent.	Die Büchse hat eine Delle.
a can of beer	eine Dose Bier
a can of paint	ein Eimer Farbe
canned/tinned food [kænd/tɪnd fuːd]	Konserve(n)
He eats a lot of canned food because it is cheaper.	Er isst viele Konserven, weil es billiger ist.
canteen [kæn'tiːn]	Kantine; Mensa
carbonated [kɑːbəneɪtəd]	kohlensäurehaltig
casserole ['kæsərəʊl]	Auflauf; Fleischeintopf
My mum makes an excellent tuna fish casserole.	Meine Mutter macht einen vorzüglichen Thunfisch-auflauf.
catering ['keɪtərɪŋ]	Lebensmittelversorgung; Catering
caviar ['kævɪɑː]	Kaviar
cereal ['sɪərɪəl]	Getreideprodukt
Cereals are good for the digestion.	Getreideprodukte sind gut für die Verdauung.
chewing-gum ['tʃuːɪŋ gʌm]	Kaugummi
I stepped in chewing-gum today.	Ich bin heute in einen Kaugummi getreten.
chicken ['tʃɪkən]	Hähnchen; Hühnchen

chicken soup ['tʃɪkən suːp]	Hühnersuppe
Chicken soup is good when you have a cold.	Hühnersuppe hilft bei Erkältung.
chips (UK) [tʃɪps]	Pommes frites
to chop [tʃɔp]	zerkleinern
Can you chop the celery, please?	Kannst du bitte den Sellerie zerkleinern?
chop [tʃɔp]	Kotelett
We are having pork chops for dinner.	Heute Abend gibt es Schweinekoteletts.
confectionery [kən'fekʃənərɪ]	Konfekt
corn [kɔːn]	Mais
Corn is my favourite vegetable.	Mais ist mein Lieblings-gemüse.
cookie (US) ['kʊkɪ]	Keks
course [kɔːs]	Gang

False Friends

Watch out!

Gang in English is not the same as *Gang* in German.

A gang in English is a *Bande* in German.

Ex: Die Bande hat einige Autos geklaut.

The gang stole several cars.

cream [kriːm]	Sahne
Can you whip the cream?	Kannst du die Sahne schlagen?

crispbread ['krɪspbred]	Knäckebrot
croissant ['krwɑːsɔŋ]	Croissant; Hörnchen
I like buttery croissants.	Ich liebe Buttercroissants.
cucumber ['kjuːkʌmbə]	Gurke
curry powder ['kʌrɪ 'paʊdə]	Currypulver
Add the curry powder to the coconut milk!	Gib das Currypulver in die Kokosmilch!
cutlery ['kʌtlərɪ]	Besteck
to defrost [diː'frɔst]	auftauen
We really need to defrost the fridge.	Wir müssen unbedingt den Kühlschrank abtauen.
delicious [dɪ'lɪʃəs]	lecker; schmackhaft
The soup was delicious.	Die Suppe war sehr lecker.
dessert [dɪ'zɜːt]	Nachspeise
We are having chocolate mousse for dessert.	Als Dessert gibt es Schokoladenmousse.
dish [dɪʃ]	Gericht; Geschirr
dough [dəʊ]	Teig
The dough needs to rise.	Der Teig muss aufgehen.
draught-beer ['drɑːftbɪə]	Fassbier
They don't have draught-beer, just bottled.	Sie haben kein Fassbier, nur Flaschen.
dumpling ['dʌmplɪŋ]	Kloß; Knödel
I love dumplings.	Ich liebe Knödel.
entrée ['ɔntreɪ]	Vorspeise
fillet ['fɪlɪt]	Filet
filleted sole	Seezungenfilet
flour [flaʊə]	Mehl

The pancakes need more flour.	Die Pfannkuchen brauchen mehr Mehl.

Homonyms

In English there are several words that are pronounced the same but spelled differently and have different meanings:
flour (Mehl): flower (Blume)
sea (Meer): see (sehen)
meat (Fleisch): meet (treffen)
flew (geflogen): flu (Grippe)
plane (Flugzeug): plain (einfach)
sun (Sonne): son (Sohn)
pray (beten): prey (Beute)
sight (Sehkraft): site (Ort)
sail (segeln): sale (Schlussverkauf)

to fold in [fəʊld ɪn]	unterziehen
fruit juice [fruːt dʒuːs]	Fruchtsaft
fruit salad [fruːt 'sæləd]	Obstsalat
She brought a fruit salad to the party.	Sie brachte einen Obstsalat zur Party mit.
to fry [fraɪ]	braten
to fry an egg	ein Spiegelei machen
garlic ['gɑːlɪk]	Knoblauch
There was a lot of garlic in the sauce.	Es war viel Knoblauch in der Soße.
to garnish ['gɑːnɪʃ]	garnieren

You can garnish the plates with parsley.	Du kannst die Teller mit Petersilie garnieren.
gravy ['greɪvɪ]	Bratensoße
The gravy is a little thick.	Die Bratensoße ist etwas dickflüssig.
to grease [griːs]	einfetten
grease [griːs]	Fett
The pizza was pretty greasy.	Die Pizza war ganz schön fettig.
hamburger patty ['hæmbɜːgə 'pætɪ]	Frikadelle; Bulette
helping ['helpɪŋ]	Portion
He took a second helping.	Er nahm eine zweite Portion.
herb [hɜːb]	Küchenkraut

Herbs in English

thyme: Thymian
basil: Basilikum
parsley: Petersilie
rosemary: Rosmarin

hot [hɔt]	warm; scharf
Be careful. The plate is hot.	Sei vorsichtig. Der Teller ist heiß.
That curry was really hot.	Der Curry war sehr scharf.
ice-cream ['aɪskriːm]	Eis
The child loves chocolate ice-cream.	Das Kind liebt Schokoladeneis.
iced coffee [aɪsd 'kɔfɪ]	Eiskaffee

ingredients [ɪn'griːdɪəntz]	Zutaten
That dish tastes best with fresh ingredients.	Dieses Gericht schmeckt mit frischen Zutaten am besten.
jam [dʒæm]	Konfitüre; Marmelade
She likes toast with jam.	Sie mag Toast mit Marmelade.
joint [dʒɔɪnt]	Keule
juice [dʒuːs]	Saft
He drinks a glass of freshly squeezed orange juice every morning.	Er trinkt jeden Morgen ein Glas frisch gepressten Orangensaft.
to knead [niːd]	kneten
lamb [læm]	Lamm
We eat lamb at Easter.	Wir essen zu Ostern Lamm.
lard [lɑːd]	Schmalz
lemonade [lemə'neɪd]	Limonade
lettuce ['letɪs]	Kopfsalat
The lettuce is wilted.	Der Kopfsalat ist verwelkt.
liver ['lɪvə]	Leber
loaf [ləʊf]	Laib
She brought a loaf of bread for dinner.	Sie brachte einen Laib Brot für das Abendessen mit.
lobster ['lɔbstə]	Hummer
Maine is famous for its lobsters.	Maine ist bekannt für seine Hummer.
main course [meɪn kɔːs]	Hauptgericht

We will be having venison as the main course.	Als Hauptgericht gibt es Hirsch.
margarine [mɑːdʒə'riːn]	Margarine
Does margarine really have less fat than butter?	Hat Margarine wirklich weniger Fett als Butter?
marinade [mærɪ'neɪd]	Marinade
The marinade is made from herbs, wine and olive oil.	Die Marinade besteht aus Kräutern, Wein und Olivenöl.
mashed potatoes [mæʃd pə'teɪtəʊz]	Kartoffelbrei
mayonnaise [meɪə'neɪz]	Majonäse
In the Netherlands, they eat chips with mayonnaise.	In den Niederlanden isst man Pommes mit Majonäse.
milkshake ['mɪlkʃeɪk]	Milchmixgetränk
mutton ['mʌtən]	Hammelfleisch
non-alcoholic [nɔn ælkə'hɔlɪk]	alkoholfrei
Do you have any non-alcoholic beverages?	Haben Sie irgendwelche alkoholfreien Getränke?
noodles ['nuːdlz]	Nudeln
nut [nʌt]	Nuss
a packet of nuts and raisins	eine Tüte Studentenfutter

Different kinds of nuts

peanuts: Erdnüsse
pistachios: Pistazien
walnuts: Walnüsse
almonds: Mandeln

nutrition [nuːˈtrɪʃən] — Ernährung
Good nutrition is important to her. — Gute Ernährung ist ihr wichtig.
off [ɔf] — verdorben; schlecht
I think the milk has gone off. — Ich glaube, dass die Milch schlecht ist.
olive oil [ˈɔlɪv ɔɪl] — Olivenöl
orange juice [ˈɔrɪndʒ dʒuːs] — Orangensaft
oven [ˈʌvən] — (Back)Ofen
The oven should be preheated. — Der Ofen sollte vorgeheizt werden.
oyster [ˈɔɪstə] — Auster
pancake [ˈpænkeɪk] — Pfannkuchen

The traditional American and English breakfasts are not very healthy! Both are very fatty, since bacon or ham and eggs form a major part of them. In the United States, another popular traditional breakfast item is pancakes, covered in butter and syrup, of course.

pastry [ˈpeɪstrɪ] — Teigwaren
pear [pɛə] — Birne
She bought a kilogram of pears. — Sie hat ein Kilo Birnen gekauft.
pork [pɔːk] — Schweinefleisch
Muslims generally do not eat pork. — Muslime essen normalerweise kein Schweinefleisch.
porridge [ˈpɔrɪdʒ] — Haferbrei; Haferschleim

potato salad [pə'teɪtəʊ 'sæləd]	Kartoffelsalat
to preserve [prɪ'zɜːv]	einkochen
preserve [prɪ'zɜːv]	Eingemachtes
She made quince preserves.	Sie machte Quitten ein.
preservative [prɪ'zɜːvətɪv]	Konservierungsstoff
to raise [reɪz]	aufgehen lassen
rancid ['rænsɪd]	ranzig
rare [rɛə]	blutig
Do you like your steak rare?	Möchtest du dein Steak blutig?
raw [rɔː]	roh; ungekocht
Sushi is raw fish.	Sushi ist roher Fisch.
recipe ['resɪpɪ]	Rezept
Could you give me the recipe for that cake?	Könntest du mir das Rezept für diesen Kuchen geben?
refreshment [rɪ'freʃmənt]	Erfrischung
refrigerator [rɪ'frɪdʒəreɪtə]	Kühlschrank
rice [raɪs]	Reis
Rice is a staple of the Asian cuisine.	Reis ist ein Grundnahrungsmittel der asiatischen Küche.
to roast [rəʊst]	braten
roast [rəʊst]	Braten
She made a wonderful roast with potatoes.	Sie hat einen ausgezeichneten Braten mit Kartoffeln gemacht.

roast beef [rəʊst biːf]	Rinderbraten
salmon ['sæmən]	Lachs
I like salmon with horse-radish.	Ich mag Lachs mit Meerrettich.
sausage ['sɔsɪdʒ]	Wurst
seafood ['siːfuːd]	Meeresfrüchte
Shrimp and crab are types of seafood.	Garnelen und Krebse sind Meeresfrüchte.
set meal [set miːl]	Menü
short-crust pastry [ʃɔːt krʌst peɪstrɪ]	Mürbteig
side-dish [saɪd dɪʃ]	Beilage
You can have potatoes or salad as a side-dish.	Du kannst entweder Kartoffeln oder Salat als Beilage haben.
sieve [sɪv]	Sieb
Where is the sieve for the noodles?	Wo ist das Sieb für die Nudeln?
to simmer ['sɪmə]	garen; köcheln
Let the sauce simmer for 15 minutes!	Lass die Sauce 15 Minuten köcheln!
slice [slaɪs]	Scheibe
I would like another slice of bread.	Ich hätte gern noch eine Scheibc Brot.
soufflé ['suːfleɪ]	Soufflé
sour ['saʊə]	sauer; herb
The lemon mousse was a bit sour.	Das Zitronenmousse war etwas sauer.

spirits ['spɪrɪts]	Spirituosen
sponge [spʌndʒ]	Biskuit
to spread [spred]	bestreichen
He spread butter on his pancakes.	Er bestrich seine Pfannkuchen mit Butter.
spread [spred]	(Brot)Aufstrich; Festessen; Festschmaus
That was an excellent spread.	Das war super, was du da aufgetischt hast.

ea as [e]

There are several words in the Englisch language where the *ea* is pronounced like a short *[e]*.

lead	Blei
read	laß (Vergangenheitsform von lesen)
dead	tot
head	Kopf

stale [steɪl]	alt; altbacken
You can use stale bread to make breadcrumbs.	Du kannst altes Brot für Semmelbrösel benutzen.
steak [steɪk]	Beefsteak
to steam [stiːm]	dampfen; dünsten
If you steam vegetables, the vitamins are retained.	Wenn du Gemüse dünstest, bleiben die Vitamine erhalten.
steam [stiːm]	Dampf

to stir [stɜː]	rühren
Risotto needs to be stirred constantly.	Risotto muss ständig gerührt werden.
James Bond likes his martini shaken, not stirred.	James Bond mag seinen Martini geschüttelt, nicht gerührt.
stock [stɔk]	Bouillon; Brühe
sweet [swiːt]	Nachspeise (UK); Süßigkeit; Bonbon
for sweet	zum Nachtisch
The children are not allowed to have sweets.	Die Kinder dürfen keine Süßigkeiten essen.
tea bag [tiː bæg]	Teebeutel
tomato [tə'mɑːtəʊ]	Tomate
tomato juice	Tomatensaft
We can use tomato paste for the pizza.	Für die Pizza können wir Tomatenmark benutzen.
tuna ['tjuːnə]	Thunfisch
veal [viːl]	Kalbfleisch
vegetable soup ['vedʒtəbl suːp]	Gemüsesuppe
wheat [wiːt]	Weizen
Wheat germ is very healthy.	Weizenkleie ist sehr gesund.
well-done [wel dʌn]	durchgebraten
The meat should be well-done.	Das Fleisch sollte durchgebraten sein.
yoghurt ['jɔgət]	Joghurt

Religion und Kirche

1. Weltreligionen

atheism ['eɪθɪɪzəm]	Atheismus
Atheists do not believe that God exists.	Atheisten glauben nicht daran, dass Gott existiert.
to believe [bɪ'liːv]	glauben
I don't know what I believe.	Ich weiß nicht, woran ich glaube.
to believe in God	an Gott glauben
belief [bɪ'liːf]	Glaube
Buddhism ['bʊdɪzəm]	Buddhismus
Buddhism is widely practised in Asia.	Der Buddhismus wird häufig in Asien gelebt.
commandment [kə'mɑːndmənt]	Gebot
There are ten important commandments in the Bible.	Es gibt in der Bibel zehn wichtige Gebote.
creation [kriː'eɪʃən]	Schöpfung
The creation lasted seven days.	Die Schöpfung dauerte sieben Tage.
devotion [dɪ'vəʊʃən]	Andacht; Frömmigkeit
to perform one's devotions	Andacht halten
divine [dɪ'vaɪn]	göttlich
They say he had divine powers.	Sie sagen, er hätte göttliche Kräfte.
eternity [ɪ'tɜːnətɪ]	Ewigkeit

There is no end to eternity.	Die Ewigkeit hat keine Begrenzung.
God [gɔd]	Gott
holy ['həʊlɪ]	heilig
Jerusalem is a holy place for both Muslims and Jews.	Jerusalem ist für Muslime und Juden eine heilige Stadt.
Islam ['ɪzlɑːm]	Islam
Judaism ['dʒuːdeɪɪzəm]	Judentum
monotheism ['mɔnəθiːɪzəm]	Monotheismus
Christianity is an example of monotheism.	Das Christentum ist ein Beispiel für Monotheismus.
pantheism ['pænθɪɪzəm]	Pantheismus
Hinduism has many gods, and therefore is pantheistic.	Der Hinduismus hat viele Götter und ist deswegen pantheistisch.
pious ['paɪəs]	andächtig; fromm
The nun was very pious.	Die Nonne war sehr fromm.
to praise [preɪs]	preisen
to pray [preɪ]	beten
She prayed that her mother would get well.	Sie betete dafür, dass ihre Mutter gesund werde.
prayer ['prɛə]	Gebet
to prophesy ['prɔfɪsaɪ]	prophezeien; voraussagen
He prophesied that the world would end in 1999.	Er prophezeite, dass der Weltuntergang 1999 stattfinden würde.

prophet ['prɔfɪt]	Prophet
Elijah was a prophet in the Old Testament.	Elijah war ein Prophet aus dem Alten Testament.
religion [rɪ'lɪdʒən]	Religion
sect [sekt]	Sekte
superstitious [suːpə'stɪʃəs]	abergläubisch

The English and Americans have strange superstitions: You will have bad luck if

1. you break a mirror.
2. you open an umbrella indoors.
3. you walk under a ladder.
4. you spill salt and do not immediately throw some of it over your left shoulder.
5. a black cat crosses your path coming from the left side.
6. you step on a crack in the pavement.

synagogue ['sɪnəgɔg]	Synagoge
The synagogue in Prage is a popular tourist attraction.	Die Synagoge in Prag ist eine beliebte Touristenattraktion.

2. Christliche Kirchen

absolution [æbsə'luːʃən]	Lossprechung; Absolution
altar ['ɔːltə]	Altar
The altar was hung with purple cloth.	Der Altar wurde mit purpurnem Stoff verhängt.

angel ['eɪndʒəl]	Engel
Angels are usually portrayed with halos and harps.	Engel werden gewöhnlich mit Heiligenschein und Harfe dargestellt.
Antichrist ['æntɪkraɪst]	Antichrist
apocalypse [ə'pɔkəlɪps]	Apokalypse; Offenbarung
apostle [ə'pɔsl]	Apostel
Peter and Thomas were apostles of Christ.	Petrus und Thomas waren Apostel Christi.
archbishop [ɑːtʃ'bɪʃəp]	Erzbischof
The archbishop was in Rome.	Der Erzbischof war in Rom.
Ascension [ə'senʃən]	Christi Himmelfahrt
baptism ['bæptɪzəm]	Taufe
They attended the child's baptism.	Sie waren bei der Taufe des Kindes dabei.
Bible ['baɪbl]	Bibel
bishop ['bɪʃəp]	Bischof
to bless [bles]	segnen
The bishop blessed the children.	Der Bischof segnete die Kinder.
cathedral [kə'θiːdrəl]	Dom; Kathedrale

False Friends

Watch out! *Dom* and the English *dome* are not the same thing. A dome is translated into German as *Kuppel*.
Ex: The dome on the cathedral was lovely.
Die Kuppel des Doms war wunderschön.

Catholicism [kə'θɔlɪsɪzəm]	Katholizismus
chapel ['tʃæpl]	Kapelle
They were married in a small chapel.	Sie haben in einer kleinen Kapelle geheiratet.
charisma [kə'rɪzmə]	Gnadengabe
Christ [kraɪst]	Christus
to christen ['krɪsn]	taufen
They christened the girl Mary.	Sie haben das Mädchen Mary getauft.
Christian ['krɪstʃən]	Christ(in); christlich
Christmas ['krɪsməs]	Weihnachten
to celebrate Christmas	Weihnachten feiern

Christmas in the USA and England

Unlike in some European countries, the 24th of December, Christmas Eve, is not the most important day. Instead, the 25th of December is when the presents are opened and the family visits.

Christmas Eve ['krɪsməs iːv]	Heiligabend
church [tʃɜːtʃ]	Kirche
church service [tʃɜːtʃ 'sɜːvɪs]	Gottesdienst
to hold a service	Gottesdienst halten
communion [kə'mjuːnɪən]	Abendmahl; Kommunion
You can not take communion unless you have been baptized.	Du kannst am Abendmahl nicht teilnehmen, wenn du nicht getauft bist.

to confess [kən'fes]	beichten
He confessed his sins to the priest.	Er beichtete dem Priester seine Sünden.
to go to confession	die Beichte ablegen
confessional	Beichtstuhl
confirmation [kɔnfə'meɪʃən]	Firmung; Konfirmation
congregation [kɔngrɪ'geɪʃən]	Gemeinde
The congregation is very welcoming to new members.	Die Gemeinde ist sehr offen für neue Mitglieder.
conversion [kən'vɜːʒən]	Bekehrung
She has been different ever since her conversion to Catholicism.	Sie hat sich seit ihrer Bekehrung zum Katholizismus verändert.
cross [krɔs]	Kreuz
The cross is an important symbol in Christianity.	Das Kreuz ist im Christentum ein wichtiges Symbol.
crucifixion [kruːsɪ'fɪkʃən]	Kreuzigung
There are many paintings of the crucifixion.	Es gibt von der Kreuzigung Jesu viele Gemälde.
devil ['devl]	Teufel
Some believe that the devil is the source of evil.	Manche glauben, dass der Teufel die Quelle des Bösen ist.
Easter ['iːstə]	Ostern
Good Friday [gʊd 'fraɪdeɪ]	Karfreitag
Are you going to church on Good Friday?	Wirst du Karfreitag in die Kirche gehen?

gospel ['gɔspəl]	Evangelium
St John's Gospel	das Johannesevangelium
grace [greɪs]	Gnade
Grace is an important virtue.	Gnade ist eine wichtige Tugend.
heresy ['herəsɪ]	Ketzerei
She was burned at the stake for heresy.	Sie wurde wegen Ketzerei auf dem Scheiterhaufen verbrannt.
hymn [hɪm]	Kirchengesang
Luther wrote many hymns.	Luther schrieb viele Kirchengesänge.
hymnbook	Gesangbuch
last rites [lɑːst raɪts]	Sterbesakramente
The last rites were performed in the hospital.	Die Sterbesakramente wurden im Krankenhaus gegeben.
to administer the last rites	die Sterbesakramente geben
liturgy ['lɪtədʒɪ]	Liturgie
Lord's Prayer [lɔːdz 'prɛə]	Vaterunser
The service always ends with the Lord's Prayer.	Der Gottesdienst endet immer mit dem Vaterunser.
mass [mæs]	Messe
to celebrate mass	die Messe halten
monastery ['mɔnəstrɪ]	Mönchskloster
He retired to a monastery.	Er zog sich in ein Mönchskloster zurück.

monk [mʌŋk]	Mönch
mortal sin ['mɔːtl sɪn]	Todsünde
Greed is a mortal sin.	Gier ist eine Todsünde.
to commit a (mortal) sin	eine (Tod)Sünde begehen
nun [nʌn]	Nonne; Ordensschwester
The nuns founded a school.	Die Nonnen gründeten eine Schule.
original sin [ə'rɪdʒɪnəl sɪn]	Sündenfall; Erbsünde
penance ['penəns]	Buße
Pentecost ['pentɪkɔst]	Pfingsten
Pentecost is a few weeks after Easter.	Pfingsten ist ein paar Wochen nach Ostern.
pilgrimage ['pɪlgrɪmɪdʒ]	Wallfahrt
to go on a pilgrimage	auf Wallfahrt gehen
The pilgrimage to Mecca is an important part of the Muslim religion.	Die Wallfahrt nach Mekka ist ein wichtiger Bestandteil des muslimischen Glaubens.
Pope [pəʊp]	Papst
The Pope held mass at St. Peter's.	Der Papst feierte die Messe im Petersdom.
to preach [priːtʃ]	predigen
He preached on the need for an end to the violence and more brotherly love.	Er predigte für ein Ende der Gewalt und die Praxis der Nächstenliebe.
priest [priːst]	Priester
Priests are not allowed to marry.	Priester dürfen nicht heiraten.

Protestant ['prɔtɪstənt]	Protestant(in)
to redeem [rɪ'diːm]	erlösen
to repent [rɪ'pent]	bereuen; Reue empfinden
to repent one's sins	seine Sünden bereuen
He repented his affair.	Er bereute seine Affäre.
resurrection [rezə'rekʃən]	Auferstehung
the resurrection from the dead	die Auferstehung von den Toten
saint [seɪnt]	Heilige(r)
a man of great sanctity	ein sehr heiliger Mann
Saviour ['seɪvjə]	Heiland
Jesus Christ is also known as the Saviour.	Christus wird auch der Heiland genannt.
sermon ['sɜːmən]	Predigt
the Sermon on the Mount	die Bergpredigt
Last week's sermon was very moving.	Die Predigt von letzter Woche war sehr anrührend.
service ['sɜːvɪs]	Gottesdienst
to hold a service	Gottesdienst halten
sin [sɪn]	Sünde
to sin against	sündigen; verstoßen
trinity ['trɪnɪtɪ]	Dreifaltigkeit
The Father, Son and Holy Spirit make up the Trinity.	Der Vater, der Sohn und der Heilige Geist bilden die Dreifaltigkeit.
vicar ['vɪkə]	Pastor

Sport

to aim [eɪm]	zielen
He aimed the arrow at the target.	Er zielte mit dem Pfeil auf die Scheibe.
amateur ['æmətə]	Amateur
He is still playing in the amateur league.	Er spielt noch immer in der Amateurliga.
aquasport ['ækwəspɔːt]	Wassersport
archery ['ɑːtʃərɪ]	Bogenschießen
William Tell is known for his archery.	Wilhelm Tell ist für sein Bogenschießen bekannt.
arrow ['ærəʊ]	Pfeil
association [əsəʊsɪ'eɪʃən]	Verband
The baseball association decided to ban him.	Der Baseballverband beschloss, ihn auszuschließen.
athlete ['æθliːt]	Athlet(in)
She is a marvellous athlete.	Sie ist eine ausgezeichnete Athletin.
athletics [æθ'letɪks]	Leichtathletik
attack [ə'tæk]	Angriff
The team started their attack.	Die Mannschaft begann ihren Angriff.
attendance [ə'tendəns]	Besucherzahl
The attendance at games has increased since the team started winning.	Seit die Mannschaft gewinnt, ist die Besucherzahl gestiegen.

backstroke [bækstrəʊk]	Rückenschwimmen
balance beam ['bæləns biːm]	Schwebebalken
She fell off the balance beam.	Sie ist vom Schwebebalken gefallen.
ball [bɔːl]	Ball
basketball ['bɑːskɪtbɔːl]	Basketball
bat [bæt]	Schläger
He was so angry he broke the bat.	Er war so wütend, dass er den Schläger zerbrach.
bike [baɪk]	Fahrrad
My bike was stolen last night.	Letzte Nacht wurde mein Fahrrad geklaut.
bit [bɪt]	Gebiss; Mundstück
(diving) board [(dəɪvɪŋ) bɔːd]	Sprungbrett
He jumped from the diving board into the pool.	Er sprang vom Sprungbrett in das Becken.
to bounce [baʊns]	prellen (Ball)
The ball bounced off the wall.	Der Ball prallte an der Wand ab.

Idiom

That's the way the ball bounces is an idiomatic way of saying *that's life* or *that's the way it goes.*

boxing ['bɔksɪŋ]	Boxen
brake [breɪk]	Bremse

The brakes failed and the car crashed.	Die Bremsen versagten und das Auto verunglückte.
breaststroke [breststrəʊk]	Brustschwimmen
Breaststroke requires a lot of energy.	Brustschwimmen erfordert viel Kraft.
buoy [bɔɪ]	Boje
butterfly ['bʌtəflaɪ]	Schmetterlingsstil
canoe [kə'nuː]	Gig; Kanu
American Indians were skilled at sailing canoes.	Indianer konnten geschickt Kanu fahren.
to canter ['kæntə]	leicht galoppieren
The horse broke into a canter.	Das Pferd fing an, leicht zu galoppieren.
captain ['kæptɪn]	Mannschaftsführer(in)
champion ['tʃæmpɪən]	Meister(in)
championship ['tʃæmpɪənʃɪp]	Meisterschaft
They won the championship two years in a row.	Sie haben die Meisterschaft zwei Jahre in Folge gewonnen.
coach [kəʊtʃ]	Mannschaftsbetreuer(in)
The coach was very angry at his team's poor performance.	Der Trainer regte sich über die mangelhafte Leistung seiner Mannschaft auf.
competition [kɔmpə'tɪʃən]	Wettkampf
course [kɔːs]	Bahn; Strecke
The course has a few hills.	Die Strecke hat ein paar Hügel.

court [kɔːt]	Feld; Spielfeld
crawl [krɔːl]	Kraulen
cycling ['saɪklɪŋ]	Radsport

Sports persons

cyclist: Radfahrer
jockey: Rennreiter
figure skater: Eiskunstläufer
runner: Läufer
racing car driver: Rennfahrer

defeat [dɪ'fiːt]	Niederlage
They took the defeat pretty hard.	Die Niederlage hat sie ziemlich mitgenommen.
defence/defense (US) [dɪ'fens]	Verteidigung
difficulty factor ['dɪfɪkəltɪ 'fæktə]	Schwierigkeitsgrad
discus ['dɪskəs]	Diskus
The discus flew a long way.	Der Diskus flog weit.
disqualification [dɪskwɔlɪfɪ'keɪʃən]	Disqualifikation
She was disqualified for cheating.	Sie wurde wegen Schummeln disqualifiziert.
diving ['daɪvɪŋ]	Wasserspringen; Tauchen
division [dɪ'vɪʒən]	Spielklasse
The team has moved into a higher division.	Die Mannschaft ist in eine höhere Klasse aufgestiegen.
draw [drɔː]	Auslosung

dress [dres]	Spielkleidung
to dribble [drɪbl]	dribbeln
He dribbled past the defence.	Er dribbelte am Verteidigungsspieler vorbei.
duration [djʊ'reɪʃən]	Spieldauer
elimination [ɪlɪmɪ'neɪʃən]	Ausscheidung
They were eliminated in the quarter final.	Sie sind im Viertelfinale ausgeschieden.
event [ɪ'vent]	Veranstaltung
exercise ['eksəsaɪz]	Übung; Gymnastik
She does leg excercises to help her knee.	Sie macht Beinübungen, um ihr Knie zu trainieren.
fair play [fɛə pleɪ]	faires Verhalten; Fair play
fencing ['fensɪŋ]	Fechten
Fencing is a very elegant sport.	Fechten ist ein sehr eleganter Sport.
field [fiːld]	Spielfeld
fight [faɪt]	Kampf
final ['faɪnl]	Endkampf; Finale
The final will be played in Liverpool.	Das Finale wird in Liverpool stattfinden.
finalist ['faɪnəlɪst]	Endspielteilnehmer(in)
finish ['fɪnɪʃ]	Zieleinlauf; Ziel
The finish is at the town hall.	Der Zieleinlauf ist am Rathaus.
foil [fɔɪl]	Florett
A foil is long and light.	Ein Florett ist lang und leicht.

football ['fʊtbɔːl]	Fußball; Football (US)
foul [faʊl]	Foul
free kick [friː kɪk]	Freistoß
The other team received a free kick after the foul.	Die andere Mannschaft bekam nach dem Foul einen Freistoß.
goal [gəʊl]	Tor
The team rejoiced after the goal.	Die Mannschaft jubelte nach dem Tor.
goal-keeper [gəʊl 'kiːpə]	Torwart
The goal-keeper caught several difficult balls.	Der Torwart hat einige schwierige Bälle gehalten.
grandstand ['grændstænd]	Tribüne
There was a fight in the grandstand.	Es gab eine Schlägerei auf der Tribüne.
grip [grɪp]	Griff
ground [graʊnd]	(Fußball)Platz
gymnasium [dʒɪm'neɪzɪəm]	Turnhalle
The cheerleaders practise in the gymnasium.	Die Cheerleader üben in der Turnhalle.
gymnastics [dʒɪm'næstɪks]	Turnen
half-time [hɑːf taɪm]	Halbzeit
The show at half-time is great.	Die Show in der Halbzeit ist gigantisch.
handstand ['hændstænd]	Handstand
header ['hedə]	Kopfball
His header bounced off the bar.	Sein Kopfball prallte am Pfosten ab.

to hit [hɪt]	schlagen; treffen
to hit one's way out of trouble	sich freischlagen; sich freiboxen
hockey ['hɔkɪ]	Feldhockey
horse-racing [hɔːs 'reɪsɪŋ]	Pferderennen
He has lost a lot of money betting on horse-racing.	Er hat viel Geld durch Pferdewetten verloren.
hunting ['hʌntɪŋ]	Jagen
The hunting season starts in two weeks.	Die Jagdsaison fängt in zwei Wochen an.
ice arena [aɪs ə'riːnə]	Eissporthalle
injury ['ɪndʒərɪ]	Verletzung
She can't play in today's game due to injury.	Aufgrund einer Verletzung spielt sie heute nicht mit.
instructor [ɪn'strʌktə]	Ausbilder; Trainer
The instructor corrected their posture.	Der Trainer korrigierte ihre Haltung.
IOC [aɪəʊsiː]	Internationales Olympisches Komitee
judge [dʒʌdʒ]	Kampfrichter(in)
judo ['dʒuːdəʊ]	Judo
to jump [dʒʌmp]	springen
The horse jumped over the obstacle.	Das Pferd sprang über das Hindernis.
jury [dʒʊərɪ]	Kampfgericht
The jury will decide if that is allowed.	Das Kampfgericht wird entscheiden, ob das erlaubt ist.

to kick off [kɪk ɔf]	den Ball anstoßen
kick-off	Anpfiff; Anstoß
lane [leɪn]	(Renn)Bahn
She stepped into the other lane.	Sie wechselte in die andere Bahn.
lap [læp]	Runde
They still have five laps to go.	Sie haben noch fünf Runden.
linesman ['laɪnzmən]	Linienrichter
long-distance [lɔŋ 'dɪstəns]	Langstrecken-; Fern-
He has been a long-distance runner for years.	Er ist seit Jahren Langstreckenläufer.
loss [lɔs]	Niederlage
marathon ['mærəθən]	Marathon
The marathon is 42 kilometres.	Der Marathon ist 42 Kilometer lang.
match [mætʃ]	Wettkampf; Spiel
We'll watch the match at her place.	Wir werden das Spiel bei ihr zu Hause anschauen.
medal ['medəl]	Medaille
She won the bronze medal.	Sie hat die Bronzemedaille gewonnen.
meet [miːt]	Veranstaltung
midfield [mɪd'fiːld]	Mittelfeld
miss [mɪs]	Fehlschuss; Misserfolg
His throw was a miss.	Sein Wurf schlug fehl.
net [net]	Netz
oar [ɔː]	Ruder

He lost an oar in the water.	Er verlor im Wasser ein Ruder.
obstacle ['ɔbstəkl]	Hindernis
There are still two more obstacles on the course.	Es gibt noch zwei weitere Hindernisse auf der Strecke.
offensive [ə'fensɪv]	Offensive
off-side [ɔf saɪd]	abseits; Abseitsstellung
Olympic Games [ə'lɪmpɪk geɪmz]	Olympische Spiele
The 2004 Olympic Games will be in Athens.	Die Olympischen Spiele 2004 finden in Athen statt.
opponent [ə'pəʊnənt]	Gegner
He beat all of his opponents.	Er hat alle seine Gegner besiegt.
out (of play) [aʊt əv plei]	im Aus
pace [peɪs]	Tempo; Schritt
I can't keep up with his fast pace.	Ich kann mit seinem schnellen Tempo nicht mithalten.
paddle ['pædl]	Paddel
pedal ['pedl]	Pedal
The pedals are hard to push.	Die Pedale sind schwer zu treten.
penalty ['penəltɪ]	Strafstoß; Elfmeter
The only goal they scored yesterday was through a penalty kick.	Das einzige Tor, das sie gestern schossen, war ein Elfmeter.

personal best ['pɜːsənal best] — persönliche Bestleistung
physical education ['fɪzɪkəl edjʊ'keɪʃən] — Sport(unterricht)

Physical education
In American high schools, students have physical education (called P.E. for short) several times a week. This is often a chance for students to get some excercise and try some more unusual sports like fencing or lacrosse. P.E. is also called gym class because the instruction often takes place in the gymnasium.

pistol ['pɪstl] — Pistole
As he moved to fire the starting shot, he dropped the pistol. — Als er gerade den Startschuss geben wollte, hat er die Pistole fallen lassen.
pitch [pɪtʃ] — Spielplatz
The angry fans threw things onto the pitch. — Die empörten Fans warfen Gegenstände auf den Platz.

placing ['pleɪsɪŋ] — Platzierung
player ['pleɪə] — Spieler(in)
Almost all of their best players are injured. — Fast alle ihrer besten Spieler sind verletzt.
polo ['pəʊləʊ] — Polo
Polo is an aristocratic sport. — Polo ist eine aristokratische Sportart.

pool [puːl]	Schwimmbecken
The water in the pool was cold.	Das Wasser im Schwimmbecken war kalt.
posture ['pɔstʃə]	Haltung
pro [prəʊ]	Profi; Berufssportler
He is a professional athlete.	Er ist Berufssportler.
He won't lose control because he's a pro.	Da er ein Profi ist, wird er die Beherrschung nicht verlieren.
punch [pʌntʃ]	Schlag
He knocked his opponent out with one punch.	Er hat seinen Gegner mit einem Schlag bewusstlos geschlagen.
quarter ['kwɔːtə]	Spielviertel
There are always commercials between the quarters.	Zwischen den Spielvierteln kommen immer Werbespots.
race [reɪs]	Rennen; Lauf
The horse race starts tomorrow at three.	Das Pferderennen fängt morgen um drei an.
The 5000 m race is his best distance.	Der 5000-m-Lauf ist seine beste Strecke.
racket ['rækɪt]	Schläger
rating ['reɪtɪŋ]	(Segel)Klasse
rebound [rɪ'baʊnd]	Rebound; Abpraller (Basketball)
record ['rekɔːd]	Rekord
to break a record	einen Rekord brechen

Basketball words

forward: Member of team that is part of the offensive and whose job it is to make baskets.
free throw: A chance to make a basket after a penalty has been committed. The person shooting has to stand at a certain distance.
3-pointer: Usually a basket only brings one point. However, if the ball is shot from a certain distance and makes a basket, the team gets three points.
travelling: A foul where the player takes more than three steps without dribbling.

referee [refə'riː]	Schiedsrichter(in)
The players argued with the referee.	Die Spieler diskutierten mit dem Schiedsrichter.
relay ['riːleɪ]	Staffellauf
She was the third runner in the relay team.	Sie war der dritte Läufer in der Staffelmannschaft.
replay ['riːpleɪ]	Wiederholungsspiel
results [rɪ'zʌlts]	Ergebnisse
What were the results of the match?	Wie waren die Spielergebnisse?
to ride [raɪd]	reiten
She learned to ride as a small child.	Sie hat das Reiten als kleines Kind gelernt.
rifle ['raɪfl]	Gewehr
He took his hunting rifle into the forest.	Er nahm sein Jagdgewehr mit in den Wald.

ring [rɪŋ]	Boxring
to row [rəʊ]	rudern
She rowed for the college team.	Sie ruderte für ihre College-Mannschaft.
rudder ['rʌdə]	Steuer
saddle ['sædl]	Sattel
The saddle did not sit well.	Der Sattel saß nicht gut.
to sail [seɪl]	segeln
He has sailed on the Atlantic Ocean.	Er ist schon auf dem Atlantik gesegelt.
to score [skɔː]	ein Tor schießen
He scored a goal for England.	Er schoss ein Tor für England.
score [skɔː]	Spielstand
What's the score?	Wie ist der Spielstand?
semi-final ['semɪ 'faɪnəl]	Halbfinale
They beat their rivals to move on into the semi-final.	Sie haben ihren Rivalen besiegt und sind ins Halbfinale gekommen.
to serve [sɜːv]	(den Ball) aufschlagen; angeben
He served the ball at 180 km/h.	Er schlug den Ball mit 180 km/h.
service ['sɜːvɪs]	Aufschlag; Angabe
Her service is weak.	Ihr Aufschlag ist schwach.
set [set]	Satz
They still have two more sets to play.	Sie haben noch zwei Sätze zu spielen.

shooting ['ʃuːtɪŋ]	Schießsport
Shooting is popular in the South.	Der Schießsport ist in den Südstaaten beliebt.
side [saɪd]	Mannschaft
skiing ['skiːɪŋ]	Skifahren
They go skiing in Colorado every year.	Sie fahren jedes Jahr nach Colorado zum Skifahren.
soccer ['sɔkə]	Fußball (UK)
Soccer is becoming increasingly popular in the United States.	Fußball wird in den USA zunehmend beliebter.
somersault ['sʌməsɔːlt]	Salto
to sprint [sprɪnt]	sprinten
He sprinted at the end.	Er sprintete am Ende.
spurt [spɜːt]	Spurt
stadium ['steɪdɪəm]	Stadion
The stadium was sold out for the final.	Das Stadion war für das Endspiel ausverkauft.
stamina ['stæmɪnə]	Stehvermögen; Ausdauer
You need a lot of stamina to run a marathon.	Du brauchst für einen Marathon viel Ausdauer.
start [stɑːt]	Start
The runners were nervous, waiting for the start.	Die Läufer waren nervös, als sie auf den Start warteten.
surfing ['sɜːfɪŋ]	Wellenreiten; Surfen
The surfing in Hawaii is very good.	Auf Hawaii kann man gut surfen.

swimming ['swɪmɪŋ]	Schwimmen
Swimming can be very tiring.	Schwimmen kann sehr ermüdend sein.
target [tɑːgɪt]	Ziel (Schießsport)
team [tiːm]	Mannschaft; Team
That is one of the best teams in the league.	Das ist eine der besten Mannschaften in der Liga.
tennis ['tenɪs]	Tennis
Germany has produced several famous tennis players.	Deutschland hat einige berühmte Tennisspieler hervorgebracht.
tie [taɪ]	Gleichstand
The first half of the game ended in a tie.	Die erste Hälfte des Spiels endete unentschieden.
track [træk]	Rennbahn
The track was a bit slippery from the rain.	Die Rennbahn war vom Regen etwas glatt.
trainer ['treɪnə]	Trainer(in); Coach
The trainer gave his team a pep talk.	Der Coach hielt eine Rede, um seine Mannschaft aufzumuntern.
umpire ['ʌmpaɪə]	Schiedsrichter(in) (Tennis)
versus ['vɜːsəs]	gegen
Tonight's match is Manchester versus Leeds.	Heute Abend spielt Manchester gegen Leeds.
victory ['vɪktərɪ]	Sieg
The team celebrated their victory.	Die Mannschaft feierte ihren Sieg.

to warm up [wɔːm ʌp] — sich einspielen; aufwärmen
It is important to warm up before exercise. — Es ist wichtig, sich vor dem Sport aufzuwärmen.
wrestling ['reslɪŋ] — Ringen
Sumo wrestling involves very fat men. — Zum Sumoringen benötigt man sehr dicke Männer.

Excercise words
gym: Fitnessstudio
weights: Hanteln
sit-ups: Bauchübungen
steam room: Dampfbad
stretching: Dehnübungen
fit: trainiert
rollerblade: inlineskaten
aerobics course: Aerobicstunde

Verkehr

accident ['æksɪdənt] — Unfall
The accident blocked the traffic for hours. — Der Unfall blockierte stundenlang den Verkehr.
aeronautics [ɛərə'nɔːtɪks] — Luftfahrt
automobile ['ɔːtəməbiːl] — Kraftwagen
His favourite automobile is a Jaguar. — Sein Lieblingsauto ist ein Jaguar.
bitumen ['bɪtjʊmən] — Bitumen; Asphalt
to brake [breɪk] — bremsen
She braked to avoid hitting the dog. — Sie bremste, um den Hund nicht zu überfahren.

brake light [breɪk laɪt]	Bremslicht
One of my brake lights has gone.	Eines meiner Bremslichter ist durchgebrannt.
brake pedal [breɪk 'pedl]	Bremspedal
He slammed on the brake pedal.	Er trat sehr fest auf das Bremspedal.
bus [bʌs]	Bus
cab [kæb]	Taxi
He is so drunk I think we should call a cab for him.	Er ist so betrunken, dass wir ein Taxi für ihn rufen sollten.
collision [kə'lɪʒən]	Zusammenstoß
The collision was between a car and a truck.	Der Zusammenstoß war zwischen einem Auto und einem LKW.
dent [dent]	Beule
When I came back from shopping, I found a large dent in my car.	Als ich vom Einkaufen zurückkam, entdeckte ich eine große Beule an meinem Auto.
detour ['diːtʊə]	Umleitung
The detour will add two miles to the trip.	Die Umleitung verlängert die Reise um zwei Meilen.
garage ['gærɑːʒ]	Garage; Tankstelle; Werkstatt
I need to take my car to the garage this week.	Ich muss mein Auto diese Woche in die Werkstatt bringen.

to indicate ['ɪndɪkeɪt]	blinken
The car is indicating but not turning.	Das Auto blinkt, biegt aber nicht ab.
indicator ['ɪndɪkeɪtə]	Blinker
motorway ['məʊtə weɪ]	Autobahn (UK)
The motorway is closed for repairs.	Die Autobahn ist wegen Reparaturen nicht befahrbar.

On the motorway ...

to drive in the fast lane	auf der Überholspur fahren
to be photographed while speeding	geblitzt werden
to stop for a break	eine Pause einlegen
to get lost	sich verfahren
to look something up on the map	etwas im Straßenatlas nachsehen

number plate ['nʌmbəpleɪt]	Nummernschild
Did you write down his number plate?	Hast du sein Nummernschild notiert?
parking space ['pɑːkɪŋ speɪs]	Parkplatz
It is difficult to find parking space in the city centre.	Es ist schwierig, einen Parkplatz in der Innenstadt zu finden.
path [pɑːθ]	Weg
The path was muddy.	Der Weg war matschig.

pavement ['peɪvmənt]	Bürgersteig
pedestrian [pɪ'destrɪən]	Fußgänger(in)
That street is a pedestrian zone.	Diese Straße ist eine Fußgängerzone.
pedestrian crossing	Fußgängerübergang
petrol ['petrəl]	Benzin
We need to put petrol in the car before leaving.	Wir müssen tanken, bevor wir losfahren.

Driving in Britain and the US

British English	*American English*
to indicate	to signal
petrol	gas
tyre	tire
puncture	flat tire
pavement	sidewalk
motorway	highway
number plate	license plate

plane [pleɪn]	Flugzeug
to go by plane	fliegen
The plane was grounded due to a technical defect.	Das Flugzeug durfte wegen eines technischen Defekts nicht starten.
puncture ['pʌŋktʃə]	Reifenpanne
The puncture kept us from being on time.	Eine Panne hat uns davon abgehalten, pünktlich zu sein.

railway ['reɪlweɪ]	Eisenbahn
registration [redʒɪ'streɪʃən]	Zulassung
The police officer wanted to see the registration.	Der Polizist wollte die Zulassung sehen.
traffic ['træfɪk]	Verkehr
Rush hour traffic is terrible!	Berufsverkehr ist schrecklich!
traffic jam ['træfɪk dʒæm]	Stau
There was a traffic jam yesterday that was five kilometres long.	Es gab gestern einen Stau, der fünf Kilometer lang war.
to be stuck in a traffic jam	im Stau stehen
seat-belt ['siːtbelt]	Sitzgurt; Sicherheitsgurt
I hope that everyone in the car ist wearing their seat-belt.	Ich hoffe, dass jeder im Auto angeschnallt ist.
skid-mark ['skɪdmɑːk]	Bremsspur
train [treɪn]	Zug
The train was diverted to Pittsburg.	Der Zug wurde nach Pittsburg umgeleitet.
tube [tjuːb]	U-Bahn (UK)
The tube was late today because the drivers were striking.	Die U-Bahn hatte heute Verspätung, weil die Fahrer gestreikt haben.
tyre [taɪə]	Reifen
burst tyre	geplatzter Reifen
wheel [wiːl]	Rad
The bike is missing a wheel.	Dem Fahrrad fehlt ein Rad.

Drive, go, ride ...

Unlike German, where the verb *fahren* is used for practically every form of transportation, there are different verbs for different situations in English:
to ride a bike: Fahrrad fahren
to drive a car: Auto fahren
to go by bus/tube: Bus/U-Bahn fahren

Wirtschaft

1. Bankwesen, Börse und Finanzen

False Friends

Watch out! *Bank* in German and *bank* in English are not always the same. The *Bank* (German) that you sit on is called a *bench* in English.
Ex: Er saß allein auf der Bank. He sat alone on the bench.

acceptance [ək'septəns]	Akzeptanz
acceptance house	Wechselbank
accountancy [ə'kaʊntənsɪ]	Buchführung; Steuerberatung
The accountancy in that company is very disorganized.	Die Buchführung in jener Firma ist sehr unorganisiert.
accounting date [ə'kaʊntɪŋ deɪt]	Abrechnungstermin

agreement [ə'griːmənt]	Vereinbarung
They reached an agreement about her salary.	Sie haben eine Vereinbarung über ihr Gehalt getroffen.
assets ['æsets]	Aktivposten
audit ['ɔːdɪt]	Buchprüfung
The audit will take place after all departments have submitted their balances.	Die Buchprüfung wird stattfinden, nachdem alle Abteilungen ihre Bilanzen abgegeben haben.
auditor ['ɔːdɪtə]	Abschlussprüfer(in)
bill [bɪl]	Rechnung
It's been two months and the bill still hasn't been paid!	Zwei Monate sind vergangen und die Rechnung wurde immer noch nicht bezahlt!
bill of exchange [bɪl əv ɪks'tʃeɪndʒ]	Wechsel
rate of exchange	Wechselkurs
boom [buːm]	Aufschwung; Hochkonjunktur
Analysts predict a boom within the next two years.	Analysten sagen innerhalb der nächsten zwei Jahre eine Hochkonjunktur voraus.
budget ['bʌdʒɪt]	Budget
There is no room in the budget for new furniture.	Neue Möbel sind im Budget nicht vorgesehen.

to go over budget	das Budget überschreiten
commission [kə'mɪʃən]	Provision; Kommission
They ask for 10% commission.	Sie verlangen 10 % Provision.

False Friends

Watch out! The German *Provision* is not the same as the English *provision*. The English *provision* can be translated as *Vorsorgemaßnahme* or *Proviant*.
Ex: He made provision for his old age.
They brought provisions for a week of camping.

compensation [kɔmpen'seɪʃən]	Abfindung; Ersatz
He received disability compensation.	Er bekam wegen seiner Berufsunfähigkeit eine Abfindung.
to receive compensation for an accident	Abfindung wegen eines Unfalls bekommen
confidential [kɔnfi'denʃəl]	vertraulich
The information is strictly confidential.	Die Informationen sind streng vertraulich.
credit ['kredɪt]	Haben; Kredit
Your credit will get better if you pay your bills on time.	Deine Bonität wird besser ausfallen, wenn du deine Rechnungen rechtzeitig zahlen würdest.
credit card ['kredɪt kɑːd]	Kreditkarte

My credit card is frozen. — Meine Kreditkarte ist gesperrt.

creditor ['kredɪtə] — Gläubiger(in)

The creditors will meet on Monday to decide the company's fate. — Die Gläubiger werden sich am Montag treffen, um über das Schicksal der Firma zu entscheiden.

currency ['kʌrənsɪ] — Währung

In which currency did they pay for the hotel? — Mit welcher Währung haben sie das Hotel bezahlt?

currency devaluation [kʌrənsɪ diːvæljʊ'eɪʃən] — Währungsverfall; Abwertung

current account ['kʌrənt ə'kaʊnt] — Girokonto

You can check your current account through Internet banking. — Du kannst dein Girokonto über Onlinebanking abfragen.

Money, money, money ...

to cash a cheque	einen Scheck einlösen
to transfer money	Geld überweisen
to withdraw an amount	einen Betrag abheben
to open a current account	ein Girokonto einrichten
to overdraw one's account	sein Konto überziehen
to have money in the bank	Geld auf der Bank haben
to withdraw money from the bank	Geld von der Bank abheben

deal [diːl]	Geschäftsabschluss
It took months, but they finally reached a deal.	Es hat Monate gedauert, aber sie haben endlich einen Geschäftsabschluss getätigt.
debenture [dɪˈbentʃə]	Anleihe
debit [ˈdebɪt]	Schuldposten; Soll
debts [detz]	Schulden
His debts amount to over 1 million pounds.	Er hat über eine Million Pfund Schulden.
to pay off debts	Schulden begleichen
to deduct [dɪˈdʌkt]	abbuchen; absetzen; abziehen
You have to deduct your personal expenses from the bill.	Du musst deine persönlichen Ausgaben von der Rechnung abziehen.
The amount was deducted from your account.	Die Summe wurde von deinem Konto abgebucht.
deduction [dɪˈdʌkʃən]	Abzug
deficit [ˈdefɪsɪt]	Defizit; Minus; Fehlbetrag
There is a deficit of 100 Euros in my account.	Ich bin mit 100 Euro im Minus.
depreciation [dɪpriːʃɪˈeɪʃən]	Entwertung; Abwertung
The real estate market has suffered from depreciation.	Der Immobilienmarkt leidet unter Abwertung.
to devalue [diːˈvæljuː]	abwerten
Brazil is going to devalue their currency.	Brasilien wird seine Währung abwerten.

discount ['dɪskaʊnt]	Diskont; Rabatt
If you pay on time, you will receive 10% discount.	Wenn Sie rechtzeitig zahlen, bekommen Sie 10 % Rabatt.
down-payment [daʊn 'peɪmənt]	Abschlagszahlung
She put a $10,000 down-payment on the house.	Sie leistete 10.000 $ Abschlagszahlung für das Haus.
due [djuː]	fällig
The sum is due at the end of the month.	Der Betrag ist am Ende des Monats fällig.
economy [iː'kɔnəmɪ]	Wirtschaft; Ökonomie
The economy is doing better than ten years ago.	Es geht der Wirtschaft besser als vor zehn Jahren.
to exchange [ɪks'tʃeɪndʒ]	wechseln
I need to exchange some money.	Ich muss etwas Geld wechseln.
exchange [ɪks'tʃeɪndʒ]	Geldwechsel
expense [ɪk'spens]	Aufwand; Kosten
I went to great expense for that campaign.	Ich habe für diese Kampagne einen hohen finanziellen Aufwand betrieben.
to expire [ɪk'spaɪə]	ablaufen (Frist; Vertrag)
The contract expires on the 15th.	Der Vertrag läuft am 15. ab.
expiry [ɪk'spaɪərɪ]	Ablauf (Frist; Vertrag)
The expiry was yesterday.	Die Ablauffrist war gestern.

finance ['faɪnæns]	Finanzwesen
Finance is a popular main subject among students.	Finanzwesen ist unter Studenten ein beliebtes Hauptfach.
financial year [faɪ'nænʃəl jɪə]	Geschäftsjahr
This year was a short financial year.	Dieses Jahr war ein kurzes Geschäftsjahr.
free of charge [friː əv tʃɑːdʒ]	unentgeltlich
That service is free of charge.	Diese Dienstleistung ist unentgeltlich.
to fund [fʌnd]	finanzieren
The foundation is funding the new building.	Die Stiftung finanziert das neue Gebäude.
fund [fʌnd]	Fonds
giro ['dʒaɪrəʊ]	Giro
GDP [dʒiː diː piː]	Bruttoinlandsprodukt
The GDP declined this year.	Das Bruttoinlandsprodukt ging in diesem Jahr zurück.
GNP [dʒiː en piː]	Bruttosozialprodukt
gross [grəʊs]	brutto
His gross annual salary is over $200,000.	Sein Bruttojahresgehalt liegt bei über 200.000 $.
income tax ['ɪnkʌm tæks]	Einkommenssteuer
She does not have to pay much income tax as she earns so little.	Sie muss nicht so viel Einkommenssteuer zahlen, da sie so wenig verdient.

to deduct something from tax	etwas von der Steuer absetzen
tax evasion	Steuerhinterziehung
free of tax	steuerfrei
tax avoidance	Steuerumgehung
installment [ɪn'stɔːlmənt]	Rate

False Friends

Watch out!

Rate in German is not the same as *rate* in English. *Die Rate* is translated as *installment*.

Ex: We will pay for the car in installments.

Wir werden das Auto in Raten abbezahlen.

To make a payment ...

to make a payment	eine Zahlung leisten
to pay in installments	in Raten zahlen
to take out a loan	einen Kredit aufnehmen
to buy something in installments	etwas auf Raten kaufen
to put a down-payment on s.th.	eine Abschlagszahlung leisten
to settle an account	eine Rechnung begleichen
to pay by cheque	mit einem Scheck bezahlen

interest ['ɪntrɪst]	Zinsen
The interest rates on the loan are very low.	Die Zinsen für das Darlehen sind sehr niedrig.

interest rates ['ɪntrɪst reɪts]	Zinssätze
The interest rates are bound to go up this year.	Die Zinssätze müssen eigentlich in diesem Jahr steigen.
inventory ['ɪnvəntrɪ]	Bestandsaufnahme; Inventur
The inventory revealed that some items were missing.	Die Bestandsaufnahme zeigte, dass einige Objekte fehlten.
to invest [ɪn'vest]	investieren
Many entrepreneurs want to invest in Chinese companies.	Einige Unternehmer möchten in chinesische Firmen investieren.
investment [ɪn'vestmənt]	Investition; Einlage
Telecommunications is usually a good investment.	Telekommunikation ist normalerweise eine gute Investition.
to make an unprofitable investment	eine Fehlinvestition machen
invoice ['ɪnvɔɪs]	Rechnung
Have you seen the invoice for the printer?	Haben Sie die Rechnung vom Drucker gesehen?
invoice clerk	Fakturist(in)
Has she been invoiced for these yet?	Hat sie dafür schon eine Rechnung bekommen?
liability [laɪə'bɪlɪtɪ]	Haftung
The liability clause in the contract is too weak.	Die Haftungsklausel im Vertrag ist zu schwach.

liable ['laɪəbl]	haftbar
The company is liable for damages.	Die Firma ist für Schäden haftbar.
loan [ləʊn]	Darlehen; Kredit
He took out a loan for his studies.	Er nahm für sein Studium ein Darlehen auf.
to raise a loan	ein Darlehen aufnehmen
lump-sum ['lʌmpsʌm]	Abschlagssumme
The amount can be paid in a lump-sum of £100.	Der Betrag kann mit einer Abschlagssumme von 100 £ bezahlt werden.
to mismanage [mɪs'mænɪdʒ]	herunterwirtschaften; abwirtschaften
The firm has been mismanaged for years.	Die Firma wird seit Jahren heruntergewirtschaftet.
net [net]	netto
net profit	Reingewinn; Nettoertrag
It costs £20 net.	Es kostet 20 £ netto.
The net profit is not so large after all.	Alles in allem ist der Reingewinn nicht so groß.
overdraft provision ['əʊvədrɑːft prə'vɪʒn]	Überziehungskredit
I have an overdraft provision of €1000.	Ich habe einen Überziehungskredit von 1000 €.
overheads ['əʊvəheds]	Gemeinkosten; Unkosten
The business' overheads are pretty high.	Die Gemeinkosten der Firma sind ziemlich hoch.

payment ['peɪmənt]	Zahlung
I can pay it off in three payments.	Ich kann es in drei Zahlungen begleichen.
to privatize ['praɪvətaɪz]	privatisieren
public/private sector	staatlicher/privater Sektor
proceeds ['prəsiːds]	Erlös
The proceeds of the benefit will go to the orphanage.	Der Erlös der Wohltätigkeitsveranstaltung wird dem Kinderheim gespendet.
profit ['prɔfɪt]	Gewinn; Profit
profit margin ['prɔfɪt 'mɑːdʒɪn]	Gewinnspanne
The profit margin is 20%.	Die Gewinnspanne beträgt 20 %.
profitable ['prɔfɪtəbl]	Gewinn bringend
That venture isn't profitable anymore.	Das Unternehmen ist nicht mehr Gewinn bringend.
to purchase ['pɜːtʃəs]	kaufen
The parts are purchased from Vietnam.	Die Teile werden in Vietnam gekauft.
purchase ['pɜːtʃəs]	Abnahme
The purchase will take place in two months.	Die Abnahme findet in zwei Monaten statt.
purchaser ['pɜːtʃɪsə]	Abnehmer(in)
The purchaser wishes to remain anonymous.	Der Abnehmer möchte anonym bleiben.
purchasing power ['pɜːtʃəsɪŋ 'paʊə]	Kaufkraft

Consumers seem to have more purchasing power this year. | Konsumenten scheinen dieses Jahr mehr Kaufkraft zu haben.

rate of exchange [reɪt əv ɪks'tʃeɪndʒ] | Wechselkurs

The rate of exchange has remained stable. | Der Wechselkurs ist konstant geblieben.

receipt [rɪ'siːt] | Quittung; Eingang

Make sure you save all of your receipts. | Schauen Sie, dass Sie alle Quittungen aufbewahren.

The goods will be sent following receipt of the payment. | Die Waren werden nach Eingang der Zahlung versandt.

to receive [rɪ'siːv] | empfangen

recession [riː'seʃən] | Abschwung; Flaute

The recession has led to a decline in consumer spending. | Die Flaute hat zu einer Veränderung des Konsumentenverhaltens geführt.

recovery [rɪ'kʌvərɪ] | Aufschwung

The economy is in recovery after 3 hard years. | Nach drei harten Jahren ist die Wirtschaft wieder im Aufschwung.

to redeem [rɪ'diːm] | einlösen

You can redeem the coupon at any store. | Du kannst den Coupon in jedem Laden einlösen.

repayment [riː'peɪmənt] | Rückzahlung

He expects repayment by the end of the year. | Er erwartet die Rückzahlung bis Ende des Jahres.

revenue ['revənjuː]	Staatseinkünfte
sales [seɪlz]	Verkauf
He is the head of sales.	Er ist der Leiter der Verkaufsabteilung.
sales figures [seɪlz 'fɪgəz]	Umsatzzahlen
The predicted sales figures do not look good.	Die prognostizierten Umsatzzahlen sehen schlecht aus.
saleable ['seɪləbəl]	absatzfähig
The product is good but not very saleable.	Das Produkt ist gut, aber nicht sehr absatzfähig.
to sell [sel]	vertreiben; verkaufen
He sold his old car for a song.	Er verkaufte sein altes Auto zum Spottpreis.
to sell at a good price	preisgünstig verkaufen
standing order ['stændiŋ 'ɔːdə]	Dauerauftrag
The company has a standing order for 100 units per month.	Die Firma hat einen Dauerauftrag von 100 Einheiten im Monat.
statement ['steɪtmənt]	Abrechnung
Did you receive your salary statement?	Haben Sie ihre Gehaltsabrechnung bekommen?
stock-exchange ['stok ɪks'tʃeɪndʒ]	Börse
The stock-exchange is located in the heart of downtown.	Die Börse befindet sich im Zentrum der Stadt.

surcharge ['sɜːtʃɑːdʒ]	Aufpreis
There will be a surcharge if delivery is late.	Es gibt einen Aufpreis für verspätete Lieferung.
surplus ['sɜːpləs]	Überschuss
They had a surplus of £20,000.	Sie hatten einen Überschuss von 20.000 £.
tax [tæks]	Steuer
tax-free [tæks friː]	steuerfrei; abgabenfrei
Donations to charity are tax-free.	Spenden an Wohltätigkeitsorganisationen sind steuerfrei.
to transact [træn'zækt]	abwickeln; abschließen
They transacted business in the hotel lobby.	Sie haben die Geschäfte im Hotelfoyer abgewickelt.
transaction [træn'zækʃən]	Abwicklung; Abschluss; Transaktion
The transaction was finalized on Monday.	Die Abwicklung wurde am Montag abgeschlossen.
transactions	Sitzungsbericht
to transfer [træns'fɜː]	abführen; überweisen
He transferred the remaining sum to my account.	Er überwies den fehlenden Betrag auf mein Konto.
trust company [trʌst 'kʌmpənɪ]	Treuhandgesellschaft
turnover ['tɜːnəʊvə]	Umsatz; Umlauf; Lagerumschlag; Personalwechsel
to increase turnover	den Umsatz steigern

Their turnover increased by 10% this year but their profit stayed the same. — Der Umsatz ist in diesem Jahr um 10 % gestiegen, aber der Gewinn ist gleich geblieben.

to withdraw [wɪð'drɔː] — abheben

He withdrew some money from the cash machine. — Er hob etwas Geld am Geldautomaten ab.

2. Industrie, Handel und Gewerbe

abattoir ['æbətwɑː] — Schlachthof

The abattoir quarter in New York is becoming trendy. — Das New Yorker Schlachthofviertel wird trendy.

agent ['eɪdʒənt] — Agent(in); Makler(in)

The agent charges 10% commission. — Die Maklerin verlangt 10 % Provision.

to apply [ə'plaɪ] — sich bewerben

She applied for several jobs in Asia. — Sie bewarb sich um verschiedene Jobs in Asien.

articles of association ['ɑːtɪkls əv əsəʊsɪ'eɪʃən] — Gesellschaftsvertrag

That is forbidden under the articles of association. — Das ist laut Gesellschaftsvertrag verboten.

bakery ['beɪəkrɪ] — Bäckerei

We could smell the fresh bread from the bakery. — Wir konnten das frische Brot aus der Bäckerei riechen.

board [bɔːd]	Vorstand
The board decided to fire him.	Der Vorstand beschloss, ihn zu entlassen.
to be elected to the board	in den Vorstand gewählt werden
branch [brɑːntʃ]	Filiale; Branche
My bank has a branch nearby.	Meine Bank hat in der Nähe eine Filiale.
brewery ['brʊərɪ]	Brauerei
The brewery had to close down.	Die Brauerei musste schließen.
butcher ['bʊtʃə]	Metzger; Fleischer
His family have been butchers for generations.	Seine Familie gehörte seit Generationen dem Metzgerberuf an.
cartel [kɑː'tel]	Kartell
The police broke up the cartel.	Die Polizei hat das Kartell zertrümmert.
certificate [sə'tɪfɪkət]	Zertifikat; Nachweis
Please provide me with a certificate of authenticity.	Könnten Sie mir einen Nachweis der Authentizität vorlegen?
Chairman of the board ['tʃɛəmən əv ðə bɔːd]	Vorstandsvorsitzender
The Chairman of the board has come under fire for poor management.	Der Vorstandsvorsitzende ist wegen schlechten Managements häufiger kritisiert worden.

Chamber of Commerce ['tʃeɪmbə əv 'kɔmɜːs]	Handelskammer
The Chamber of Commerce can advise you in that matter.	Die Handelskammer kann dich in dieser Angelegenheit beraten.
client ['klaɪənt]	Auftraggeber(in); Klient(in)
The new company already has several established clients.	Die neue Firma hat bereits einige etablierte Auftraggeber.
The lawyer refused to comment to protect his client.	Der Anwalt verweigerte jeglichen Kommentar, um seinen Mandanten zu schützen.
commercial [kɔm'ɜːʃəl]	kaufmännisch; kommerziell
commercial agent [kɔm'ɜːʃəl 'eɪdʒənt]	Handelsvertreter(in)
We need a commercial agent for Tunesia.	Wir brauchen einen Handelsvertreter für Tunesien.
commodity [kə'mɔdɪtɪ]	Artikel; Produkt
common market ['kɔmən 'mɑːkɪt]	Binnenmarkt
to compete [kɔm'piːt]	konkurrieren
Those two companies are competing for a larger market share.	Diese zwei Firmen konkurrieren um einen größeren Marktanteil.
competition [kɔmpə'tɪʃən]	Konkurrenz
a spirit of competition	Konkurrenzdenken

False Friends

Watch out!

Concurrence does not mean the same thing as *Konkurrenz. Concurrence* translated into German means *Einklang*.

Ex: He brought their ideas into concurrence with one another.

Er brachte ihre Ideen miteinander in Einklang.

consumer [kən'sjuːmə]	Verbraucher(in)
Consumers have been complaining about high prices.	Die Verbraucher haben sich über die hohen Preise beklagt.
consumer protection [kən'sjuːmə prɔtekʃən]	Verbraucherschutz
contract ['kɔntrækt]	Vertrag
Her contract will run out at the end of the year.	Ihr Vertrag wird zum Ende des Jahres auslaufen.
contractor [kɔn'træktə]	Auftragnehmer(in)
delicatessen [delɪkə'tesən]	Feinkostladen
That delicatessen is famous for its bagels.	Dieser Feinkostladen ist für seine Bagels berühmt.

In the US, delicatessens, or delis as they are commonly known, are a popular place to grab lunches of bagels and sandwiches and to buy fresh meats and cheeses.

demand [dɪ'mɑːnd]	Nachfrage

The current supply is unable to meet the enormous demand.	Das jetzige Angebot kann die riesige Nachfrage nicht befriedigen.
to dissolve [dɪ'zɔlv]	(Firma) auflösen
The company was dissolved and the employees laid off.	Die Firma wurde aufgelöst und die Mitarbeiter entlassen.
distillery [dɪs'tɪlərɪ]	Brennerei
distribution [dɪstrɪ'bjuːʃən]	Vertrieb; Verteilung
We need to improve our distribution.	Wir müssen unseren Vertrieb verbessern.
The distribution of wealth is very unfair.	Die Verteilung des Wohlstands ist sehr ungerecht.
dry-cleaner's [draɪ 'kliːnəz]	chemische Reinigung
I will have to take the dress to the dry-cleaner's.	Ich muss das Kleid in die Reinigung bringen.
to export [ɪk'spɔːt]	exportieren; ausführen
Japan exports automobiles.	Japan exportiert Autos.
export ['ɛkspɔːt]	Export
Rice is one of that country's largest exports.	Reis ist einer der wichtigsten Exportartikel dieser Länder.
firm [fɜːm]	Firma
florist's ['flɔrɪstz]	Blumenladen
He went to the florist's to inquire about a wreath.	Er ist zum Blumenladen gegangen, um nach einem Kranz zu schauen.
food industry [fuːd 'ɪndəstrɪ]	Lebensmittelindustrie

The food industry has suffered from the BSE crisis.	Die Lebensmittelindustrie litt unter der BSE-Krise.
freight [freɪt]	Fracht
Freight is included in the price.	Fracht ist im Preis inbegriffen.
grocery ['grəʊsərɪ]	Lebensmittelgeschäft
I bought an avocado at the grocery.	Ich habe im Lebensmittelgeschäft eine Avocado gekauft.
headquarters ['hedkwɔːtəs]	Firmensitz
Their headquarters are in Shanghai.	Der Hauptsitz der Firma ist in Shanghai.
holding company ['həʊldɪŋ 'kʌmpənɪ]	Dachgesellschaft
to import [ɪm'pɔːt]	importieren; einführen
import ['ɪmpɔːt]	Import; Einfuhr
inquiry [ɪn'kwaɪrɪ]	Nachfrage; Erkundigung
Thank your for your inquiry about our products.	Vielen Dank für Ihre Anfrage bezüglich unserer Produkte.
laundrette [lɔːn'dret]	Waschsalon
I don't have a washing machine, so I have to go to the laundrette.	Ich habe keine Waschmaschine, also muss ich zum Waschsalon gehen.
limited partnership ['lɪmɪtəd 'pɑːtnəʃɪp]	Kommanditgesellschaft
liquidation [lɪkwɪ'deɪʃən]	Liquidation
market ['mɑːkɪt]	Markt; Absatzmarkt

The market for cars is booming in Asia.	In Asien boomt der Markt für Autos.
market research ['mɑːkɪt rɪ'sɜːtʃ]	Marktforschung
They invest a lot of money in market research.	Sie investieren viel Geld in Marktforschung.
marketing ['mɑːkɪtɪŋ]	Marketing; Absatzpolitik
Their marketing strategy has been successful.	Ihre Marketingstrategie hat sich als richtig erwiesen.
member of the board [membə əv ðə bɔːd]	Vorstandsmitglied
The members of the board agreed to take a salary cut.	Die Vorstandsmitglieder stimmten einer Gehaltsreduzierung zu.
market share ['mɑːkɪt ʃɛə]	Marktanteil
Their market share increased by 5%.	Ihr Marktanteil ist um 5 % gestiegen.
to operate ['ɔpəreɪt]	arbeiten; funktionieren
operating ['ɔpəreɪtɪŋ]	Betriebs-
Have you seen the operating instructions?	Hast du die Bedienungsanleitung gesehen?
to order ['ɔːdə]	bestellen
We would like to order ten new office chairs.	Wir möchten gerne zehn neue Bürostühle bestellen.
order ['ɔːdə]	Bestellung
We are calling about your order.	Wir rufen wegen Ihrer Bestellung an.
order form ['ɔːdə fɔːm]	Bestellschein

Please fill out the order form.	Bitte füllen Sie den Bestellschein aus.
partner ['pɑːtnə]	Partner(in); Teilhaber(in)
Two of the partners left the company.	Zwei Teilhaber haben die Firma verlassen.
partnership ['pɑːtnəʃɪp]	Partnerschaft; Personengesellschaft
to enter into a partnership	in eine Gesellschaft eintreten
pay [pei]	Bezahlung; Gehalt
What's the pay like?	Wie ist die Bezahlung?
It comes out of my pay.	Es wird mir vom Gehalt abgezogen.
to get paid	seinen Lohn/sein Gehalt bekommen
public limited company (plc) [piː el siː]	Aktiengesellschaft
retailer ['riːteɪlə]	Einzelhändler; Kleinhändler
Retailers enjoy increased profits at Christmas.	Einzelhändler machen zur Weihnachtszeit einen steigenden Gewinn.
retail trade ['riːteɪl treɪd]	Einzelhandel
to run [rʌn]	betreiben
They run five restaurants and three hotels.	Sie betreiben fünf Restaurants und drei Hotels.
sector ['sektə]	Sektor; Branche
The steel sector has been doing poorly.	Die Stahlbranche schneidet zurzeit schlecht ab.

to strike [straɪk]	streiken
The factory workers went on strike for higher wages.	Die Fabrikarbeiter streikten, um mehr Gehalt zu bekommen.
strike [straɪk]	Streik; Ausstand
The workers began striking on Monday.	Die Arbeiter traten am Montag in den Streik.
subsidiary [səb'sɪdɪərɪ]	Tochtergesellschaft
That company has subsidiaries on three continents.	Diese Firma hat auf drei Kontinenten Tochtergesellschaften.
supervisory board ['suːpəvaɪzərɪ bɔːd]	Aufsichtsrat
A professor of economics is a member of the supervisory board.	Ein Wirtschaftsprofessor ist Mitglied des Aufsichtsrates.
to trade [treɪd]	handeln
He trades in precious textiles.	Er handelt mit wertvollen Textilien.
trade [treɪd]	Handel; Gewerbe
That trade has enjoyed a lot of respect.	Dieses Gewerbe genießt viel Respekt.
transfer ['trænsfɜː]	Überweisung
transit ['trænsɪt]	Durchfahrt; Transit
The goods were damaged in transit.	Die Waren wurden beim Transport beschädigt.
unemployed [ʌnɪm'plɔɪd]	arbeitslos
the unemployed	die Arbeitslosen

He was unemployed for two years before finding a new job.	Bevor er einen neuen Job gefunden hat, war er zwei Jahre arbeitslos.
to receive unemployment benefit	Arbeitslosenunterstützung beziehen
to be out of work	arbeitslos sein
wholesale trade ['həʊlseɪl treɪd]	Großhandel
wholesaler ['həʊlseɪlə]	Großhändler
He buys wine from a wholesaler because it's cheaper.	Er kauft Wein vom Großhändler, weil es billiger ist.